William E. Studwell
Bruce R. Schueneman

State Songs of the United States:
An Annotated Anthology

State Songs of the United States: An Annotated Anthology
has been co-published simultaneously as *Music Reference
Services Quarterly*, Volume 6, Numbers 1/2 1997.

State Songs of the United States:
An Annotated Anthology

State Songs of the United States: An Annotated Anthology has been co-published simultaneously as *Music Reference Services Quarterly*, Volume 6, Numbers 1/2 1997.

The *Music Reference Services Quarterly* Monographs/"Separates"

Foundations in Music Bibliography, edited by Richard D. Green

Minor Ballet Composers: Bibliographical Sketches of Sixty-Six Underappreciated Yet Significant Contributors to the Body of Western Ballet Music, edited by Bruce R. Schueneman and William E. Studwell

State Songs of the United States: An Annotated Anthology, William E. Studwell and Bruce R. Schueneman

These books were published simultaneously as special thematic issues of *Music Reference Services Quarterly* and are available bound separately. Visit Haworth's website at http: / /www.haworth.com to search our online catalog for complete tables of contents and ordering information for these and other publications. Or call 1-800-HAWORTH (outside US/Canada: 607-722-5857), Fax: 1-800-895-0582 (outside US/Canada: 607-771-0012), or e-mail getinfo@ haworth.com

State Songs of the United States: An Annotated Anthology

Compiled by

William E. Studwell
and Bruce R. Schueneman

Songs assembled and revised by Bruce R. Schueneman

State Songs of the United States: An Annotated Anthology has been co-published simultaneously as *Music References Services Quarterly*, Volume 6, Numbers 1/2 1997.

The Haworth Press, Inc.
New York • London

State Songs of the United States: An Annotated Anthology has been co-published simultaneously as *Music Reference Services Quarterly,* Volume 6, Numbers 1/2 1997.

ISBN 0-7890-0397-X

The development, preparation, and publication of this work has been undertaken with great care. However, the publisher, employees, editors, and agents of The Haworth Press and all imprints of The Haworth Press, Inc., including The Haworth Medical Press and Pharmaceutical Products Press, are not responsible for any errors contained herein or for consequences that may ensue from use of materials or information contained in this work. Opinions expressed by the author(s) are not necessarily those of The Haworth Press, Inc.

Cover design by Thomas J. Mayshock Jr.

The Haworth Press, Inc., 10 Alice Street, Binghamton, NY 13904-1580 USA

Library of Congress Cataloging-in-Publication Data is not available for musical scores

INDEXING & ABSTRACTING

Contributions to this publication are selectively indexed or abstracted in print, electronic, online, or CD-ROM version(s) of the reference tools and information services listed below. This list is current as of the copyright date of this publication. See the end of this section for additional notes.

- ***CNPIEC Reference Guide: Chinese National Directory of Foreign Periodicals***, P.O. Box 88, Beijing, Peoples Republic of China

- ***IBZ International Bibliography of Periodical Literature***, Zeller Verlag GmbH & Co., P.O.B. 1949, d-49009 Osnabruck, Germany

- ***Information Science Abstracts***, Plenum Publishing Company, 233 Spring Street, New York, NY 10013-1578

- ***Informed Librarian, The***, Infosources Publishing, 140 Norma Road, Teaneck, NJ 07666

- ***International Index to Music Periodicals***, Chadwyck-Healey, Inc., 1101 King Street, Suite 380, Alexandria, VA 22314-2944

- ***INTERNET ACCESS (& additional networks) Bulletin Board for Libraries ("BUBL"), coverage of information resources on INTERNET, JANET, and other networks***.
    - <URL:http://bubl.ac.uk/>
    - The new locations will be found under <URL:http://bubl.ac. uk/link/>.
    - Any existing BUBL users who have problems finding information on the new service should contact the BUBL help line by sending e-mail to <bubl@bubl.ac.uk>.
  The Andersonian Library, Curran Building, 101 St. James Road, Glasgow G4 0NS, Scotland

- ***Library & Information Science Abstracts (LISA)***, Bowker-Saur Limited, Maypole House, Maypole Road, East Grinstead, West Sussex RH19 1HH, England

- ***Library Literature***, The H.W. Wilson Company, 950 University Avenue, Bronx, NY 10452

(continued)

- *Music Index, The,* Harmonie Park Press, 23630 Pinewood, Warren, MI 48091

- *Newsletter of Library and Information Services,* China Sci-Tech Book Review, Library of Academia Sinica, 8 Kexueyuan Nanlu, Zhongguancun, Beijing 100080, People's Republic of China

- *RILM Abstracts of Music Literature,* City University of New York, 33 West 42nd Street, New York, NY 10036

SPECIAL BIBLIOGRAPHIC NOTES

related to special journal issues (separates)
and indexing/abstracting

☐ indexing/abstracting services in this list will also cover material in any "separate" that is co-published simultaneously with Haworth's special thematic journal issue or DocuSerial. Indexing/abstracting usually covers material at the article/chapter level.

☐ monographic co-editions are intended for either non-subscribers or libraries which intend to purchase a second copy for their circulating collections.

☐ monographic co-editions are reported to all jobbers/wholesalers/approval plans. The source journal is listed as the "series" to assist the prevention of duplicate purchasing in the same manner utilized for books-in-series.

☐ to facilitate user/access services all indexing/abstracting services are encouraged to utilize the co-indexing entry note indicated at the bottom of the first page of each article/chapter/contribution.

☐ this is intended to assist a library user of any reference tool (whether print, electronic, online, or CD-ROM) to locate the monographic version if the library has purchased this version but not a subscription to the source journal.

☐ individual articles/chapters in any Haworth publication are also available through the Haworth Document Delivery Service (HDDS).

State Songs of the United States: An Annotated Anthology

CONTENTS

SONG TEXTS

ALL HAWORTH BOOKS AND JOURNALS
ARE PRINTED ON CERTIFIED
ACID-FREE PAPER

William E. Studwell, MA, MSLS, is Professor and Principal Cataloger at the University Libraries of Northern Illinois University in DeKalb. The author of *The Americana Song Reader* (The Haworth Press, Inc., 1997), Mr. Studwell is the author of nine other books on music including reference books on popular songs, state songs, ballet, and opera. He has also written three books on cataloging and almost 300 articles in library science and music. A nationally known expert on carols, college fight songs, and Library of Congress subject headings, he has made approximately 300 radio, television, and print appearances in national, regional, and local media. Mr. Studwell is the Editor of *Music Reference Services Quarterly* (The Haworth Press, Inc.) and co-editor of the book *Minor Ballet Composers* (The Haworth Press, Inc., 1997).

Bruce R. Schueneman, MLS, MS, is Head of Collection Services at Texas A&M University in Kingsville, Texas. A violinist, he studied for eleven years with Thomas Pierson. Mr. Schueneman has a special interest in the French School composers. He has published a book and several articles on Pierre Rode, one of the leading French School composers. He has also penned a series of articles on minor composers. He is currently working on the preparation of new editions of a quartet by Rode and a sonata by the American composer Cecil Burleigh and is the co-editor of the book *Minor Ballet Composers* (The Haworth Press, Inc., 1997).

Preface

All but four states of the United States (Michigan, New Jersey, New York, and Virginia) have one or more official state songs. In addition, some states have songs which are closely associated with them yet are not official representatives of the jurisdictions. This volume combines both official and non-official state songs into one convenient volume. All 50 states are represented in some way, sometimes by one song, and sometimes by two or three. The selection criteria included availability, quality, familiarity, and the obvious necessity to cover all the states.

If permission to publish a song was obtained, or if a song is in public domain, the text of the song, words and music, is published (sometimes with a new arrangement) and with an historical annotation. Of the 69 songs included in this anthology, 48 have both the song text and an historical note. The remaining 21 songs, for which permission to publish the text could not be obtained, are covered only by historical data. When entire song texts are presented, the historical note includes all verses; the text (words and music) contains only one verse, almost always the first. Although it would of course have been preferable to publish the texts for all involved songs, the compilers feel that since there is a real need for a scholarly and well-arranged collection of state songs, a somewhat incomplete anthology is better than a non-existent one.

A fair proportion of the songs reproduced or mentioned in this volume are also known in other contexts than that of a state song and/or are well known for one reason or another. These include "The Arkansas Traveler," "Beautiful Ohio," "California, Here I Come," "Carry Me Back to Old Virginia," "The Eyes of Texas,"

[Haworth co-indexing entry note]: "Preface." Studwell, William E., and Bruce R. Schueneman. Co-published simultaneously in *Music Reference Services Quarterly* (The Haworth Press, Inc.) Vol. 6, No. 1/2, 1997, pp. xv-xviii; and: *State Songs of the United States: An Annotated Anthology* (William E. Studwell, and Bruce R. Schueneman) The Haworth Press, Inc., 1997, pp. xv-xviii. Single or multiple copies of this article are available for a fee from The Haworth Document Delivery Service [1-800-342-9678, 9:00 a.m. - 5:00 p.m. (EST). E-mail address: getinfo@haworth.com].

xv

"Georgia on My Mind," "Home on the Range," "Indiana," "Iowa Corn Song," "Maryland! My Maryland," "Missouri Waltz," "My Old Kentucky Home," "Old Folks at Home," "Oklahoma," "On the Banks of the Wabash," "On, Wisconsin," "The Sidewalks of New York," "Tennessee Waltz," and "Yankee Doodle." The majority of the songs, however, are not well known and are seldom published. That is the primary reason for this volume.

The state songs of the United States are a mixed lot. For the most part they represent popular music of the late 19th and early 20th centuries. Some are well-known songs that happen to mention the name of a state (the two Stephen Foster songs, for example), others are the result of contests specifically designed to solicit an official state song (and therefore tend to be highly patriotic), others derive from Broadway ("Oklahoma!") or recent popular music ("Georgia on My Mind"), still others are sentimental ballads reflecting a love of home. Some songs have a reverent hymn-like quality (and many mention God), while others are folk songs (such as "The Arkansas Traveler").

The songs mirror American attitudes about the numerous places Americans call home. Most songs are rural in the sense that the natural physical characteristics are described; cities are only rarely mentioned. History is not forgotten either. While this is usually expressed in vague terms, in several instances the entire song concerns an historic event. Both "Maryland, My Maryland" and "Carolina" were born in the Civil War and cannot be understood outside the context of Civil War times. References to "Northern scum" and "huns" make these songs even more historical period pieces than is usually the case with state songs.

Racial attitudes of the period are also evident in many lyrics. Today these lyrics are offensive to most Americans as are the attitudes they express. The editors have changed the lyrics in several places: the "darkies" of the Stephen Foster songs has been changed to "dear ones" or "people" and the language has been cast in standard English. The original lyrics of "The Yellow Rose of Texas" assume the persona of a "darkey" and describe the charms of the "yellow rose of color." Northern songs are not immune from this problem. "My Michigan" also contains the word "darkies" in describing the maidens of Alabama. The "dusky" maidens of Idaho are also deemed inferior to the Michigan (presumably light-skinned) variety. The states themselves have sometimes recognized this problem. Florida officially changed the lyrics of Foster's "Old Folks at Home" in the late 1970s.

The most problematic song in this regard is "Carry Me Back to Old Virginny." In January 1997 Virginia, after a long legislative battle, repudiated its long time state song. (The original title, "Carry Me Back to Old Virginny," was amended to "Carry Me Back to Old Virginia" when the state adopted the song in 1940.) One suggestion was to clean up the song by making several word changes. The song depicts an ex-slave (in 1878) thinking fondly of old Virginia and his old massa. The suggested word changes made it appear that the song is not a slave's longing for the old slavery days but a sentimental general nostalgia for old Virginia (the time period left vague). This suggestion was voted down by the Virginia legislature. The song's repudiation was not complete, however, and "Carry Me Back to Old Virginia" is now styled the state song emeritus, an interesting and novel category. Only time will tell if Virginia's solution is followed by other states. It is perhaps ironic that the words from one of the few state songs by an African American lyricist are now considered too racist to use as a state song.

Another interesting example of racial attitudes in state songs is "Missouri Waltz." The original 1914 lyrics used the words "picka-ninnies" and "mammy." In a later 1945 printing (that is identical except for the word changes and the cover of the sheet music which identifies it as the official state song) these words are replaced by "old folks" and "Mommy." These word changes, like the ones contemplated for "Carry Me Back to Old Virginia," change the entire context of the song. Instead of a black mammy singing a baby to sleep and dreaming of Dixieland, the persona becomes white, or at least of indeterminate race. The longing for Dixie, though, re-mains intact.

These songs also mirror their times in regard to the treatment of women. In the Michigan song mentioned above, the lyricist compares varieties of women as if they were bottles of wine and discovers (no surprise here!) that Michigan women are best. Other songs also speak of women in the same terms as the natural world, almost as if women were inanimate physical things like mountains or lakes.

Despite their faults and historical datedness, these songs represent a fascinating portrait of America. These songs can be enjoyed for themselves, and several are gems of American popular music. Jingoistic, passionate, and sentimental by turns, they represent what Americans thought–and still think–of themselves. In that light they are also important historical documents.

William E. Studwell
Bruce R. Schueneman

Acknowledgments

Grateful acknowledgment is made to the following states and organizations for permission to reprint the words and music to the indicated state songs:

The State of Arkansas for permission to use "Arkansas."

Delaware State Archives for permission to use "Our Delaware."

The University of Idaho for permission to use "Here We Have Idaho."

The State of Maine for permission to use "State of Maine."

The University of Minnesota Alumni Association for permission to use "Hail! Minnesota."

The Shodair Children's Hospital for permission to use "Montana."

The Willis Music Company for permission to use "Beautiful Nebraska."

The State of North Carolina for permission to use "The Old North State."

The State of South Dakota for permission to use "Hail! South Dakota."

The State of Washington for permission to use "Washington My Home."

Bailey School and Office Supply for permission to use "Wyoming."

A Tribute to American Song

State Songs of the United States is the first of three volumes of similar style and intent. All three volumes will present texts of and basic historical information on compositions which are collectively significant elements in American culture, even if individually they may not be well-known or widely-used. All represent musical lacunae or cultural backwaters which have not received a lot of attention from either historians or anthologists. Yet all three bodies of song are to some degree familiar to many Americans in the course of their year in and year out living, working, and recreating. They are not everyday songs like national anthems, hymns, popular songs, television themes and advertising jingles, and childrens' ditties such as "Happy Birthday to You," yet at the same time they are not esoteric or far removed from the cultural mainstream.

In the present volume of state songs, the reader will find some compositions which are very familiar, some which are fairly familiar, and some which are quite obscure. In at least a few cases, the state song may not be even well-known in its particular jurisdiction. A somewhat opposite scenario is associated with the second expected annotated Americana anthology, *College Fight Songs*. Most persons who are students or staff on the campuses of American universities and colleges and who participate in or attend campus sporting events and various other local occasions are familiar with at least one of the school's fight songs. There are probably few institutions of higher learning in the United States that do not have some type of fight or sports song to cheer on the athletic teams and to generally promote the organization. However, most college fight songs are rarely heard outside the campus of their origins and the

[Haworth co-indexing entry note]: "A Tribute to American Song." Studwell, William E. Co-published simultaneously in *Music Reference Services Quarterly* (The Haworth Press, Inc.) Vol. 6, No. 1/2, 1997, pp. 1-15; and: *State Songs of the United States: An Annotated Anthology* (William E. Studwell, and Bruce R. Schueneman) The Haworth Press, Inc., 1997, pp. 1-15. Single or multiple copies of this article are available for a fee from The Haworth Document Delivery Service [1-800-342-9678, 9:00 a.m. - 5:00 p.m. (EST). E-mail address: getinfo@haworth.com].

stadiums and arenas athletic teams visit in the course of intercollegiate competition.

The third expected anthology, *Circus Songs,* has yet another type of scenario. With some exceptions, songs specifically written for the circus or widely adopted by circus musicians are only performed when "the greatest show on earth" and similar popular gaudy and exciting events are taking place. Carnivals, fancily decorated carousels, exhibitions of weird and bizarre phenomena, girlie shows, and other occasions on the titillating fringe of society are also frequent dispensers of circus-style musical compositions.

These three anthologies, one relating to American government, one relating to American higher education, and one relating to popular amusements, though collectively dealing with a sizeable portion of American life, only cover a relatively small amount of the huge body of American and foreign music which has soothed, comforted, amused, excited, and inspired Americans for centuries. Americans have made notable contributions in many areas of music, including "classical" or "serious music," but what American composers and performers have excelled in most is the creation of a huge amount of shorter pieces we call songs. Whether the song is patriotic, romantic, religious, humorous, calm, stimulating, fast, slow, in older modes like the waltz, or in the newer modes of jazz or rock and roll (both American innovations), or whether the song was from Tin Pan Alley or Broadway in New York, or the rural areas of the South or the West, or from black clubs of New Orleans, or someplace else, Americans have produced an almost countless number of good and/or successful songs in the past two centuries or so. Largely because of jazz and rock and roll, American songs, like so many other artistic, technological, intellectual, or commercial products from the United States, have become an influential and widespread cultural force in the twentieth century.

As an adjunct to this song anthology and the two other expected Americana collections, it seems appropriate to present an appreciation for the long term wealth of American song. Therefore, 221 noteworthy American songs are listed chronologically below. Why 221? Well, it has been 221 years since the Declaration of Independence was signed, and accordingly the upcoming list could be regarded as sort of a declaration of some of the musical achievements of the United States. The list is of course very subjective. It includes a number of obvious choices as well as a number of more debatable selections. Most of the songs are totally American, some are partially American, and some are suspected to be American. When the lyrics and melodies are known to have been created at different times, the song is listed under the first of the dates. When the song is a mix of American and foreign elements, the piece is listed under the date of the American component.

Altogether, the list is intended to at least partially mirror the changing American cultural scene up to the early 1970s. Therefore, the reader will find a broad spectrum of classics, interesting compositions, and old favorites presented. Of course, a large number of good songs will not be on the list since there are literally thousands to select from. Variety is the key. Since all the songs listed have to have endured for at least one generation past their creation or popularization, the early 1970s are a necessary cutoff time. Although the list covers over two centuries of varied musical endeavor, it should be noted that both the chronologically first and chronologically last, "The Girl I Left Behind Me" and "Jesus Christ, Superstar," reflect the age old themes of romance and religion. Things are always changing, yet tend to repeatedly cover similar ground over and over again.

Finally, here is the main point of this essay, the listing of the 221 honored songs:

TO 1860

"The Girl I Left Behind Me" (wm. anonymous, 1760s)

"Yankee Doodle" (wm. anonymous, probably Francis Hopkinson, 1760s?)

"Hail to the Chief" (w. Scotsman Walter Scott, 1810, m. anonymous, 1812)

"The Star-Spangled Banner" (w. Francis Scott Key, 1814, m. anonymous English, around 1779)

"Home Sweet Home" (w. John Howard Payne, m. Englishman Henry Rowley Bishop, 1823)

"Amazing Grace" (w. Englishman John Newton, 1779, m. anonymous, 1831)

"America" ("My Country 'Tis of Thee") (w. Samuel Francis Smith, 1832, m. anonymous English, 1744)

"Turkey in the Straw" (w. anonymous, 1861, m. anonymous, 1834)

"She Wore a Yellow Ribbon" (wm. anonymous, 1838)

"Joy to the World" (w. Englishman Isaac Watts, 1719, m. Lowell Mason, 1839)

"Columbia, the Gem of the Ocean (wm. anonymous, 1843)

"Buffalo Gals" (wm. Cool White, 1844)

"Oh, Susanna" (wm. Stephen Foster, 1847)

"Camptown Races" (wm. Stephen Foster, 1850)

"Old Folks at Home" ("Swanee River") (wm. Stephen Foster, 1851)

"My Old Kentucky Home, Good Night!" (wm. Stephen Foster, 1853)

"Listen to the Mocking Bird" (wm. Septimus Winner, 1855)

"Nearer, My God to Thee" (w. Englishwoman Sarah F. Adams, 1841, m. Lowell Mason, 1856)

"Jingle Bells" (wm. James S. Pierpont, 1857)

"We Three Kings of Orient Are" (wm. John Henry Hopkins, 1857)

"Far Above Cayuga's Waters" (w. Archibald W. Weeks, Wilmot M. Smith, 1872, m. H. S. Thompson, 1858)

"Yellow Rose of Texas" (wm. anonymous, 1858)

"Dixie" (wm. Daniel Decatur Emmett, 1859)

"Simple Gifts" (m. anonymous, probably before 1860)

"Swing Low, Sweet Chariot" (wm. anonymous, probably before 1860)

1860-1899

"Battle Hymn of the Republic" (w. Julia Ward Howe, 1862, m. anonymous, 1850s?)

"When Johnny Comes Marching Home (wm. Patrick Gilmore, 1863)

"Beautiful Dreamer" (wm. Stephen Foster, 1864)

"The Little Brown Church in the Vale" (wm. William Savage Pitts, 1865)

"Old Time Religion" (wm. anonymous, published 1865)

"O Little Town of Bethlehem" (w. Phillips Brooks, m. Lewis H. Redner, 1868)

"Little Brown Jug" (wm. Joseph Eastburn Winner, 1869)

"Rock-a-Bye Baby" (wm. Effie I. Crockett, around 1872)

"Home on the Range" (w. probably Brewster M. Higley, 1873, m. probably Daniel E. Kelley, 1904)

"God of Our Fathers" (w. Daniel C. Roberts, 1876, m. George W. Warren, 1894)

"Carry Me Back to Old Virginny" (wm. James A. Bland, 1878)

"Row, Row, Row Your Boat" (wm. anonymous, 1881)

"America the Beautiful" (w. Katharine Lee Bates, 1893, m. Samuel A. Ward, 1882)

"There Is a Tavern in the Town" (wm. anonymous, 1883)

"Clementine" (wm. anonymous 1884)

"While Strolling Through the Park One Day" (wm. Robert A. King, 1884)

"American Patrol" (m. Frank W. Meacham, 1885)

"Semper Fidelis" (m. John Philip Sousa, 1888)

"The Washington Post March" (m. John Philip Sousa, 1889)

"After the Ball" (wm. Charles K. Harris, 1892)

"Happy Birthday to You" (w. Patty Smith Hill, m. Mildred J. Hill, 1893)

"The Whiffenpoof Song" (w. Meade Minnigerode, George S. Pomeroy, 1909, m. probably Guy H. Scull, around 1893)

"I've Been Working on the Railroad" (wm. anonymous, 1894)

"The Sidewalks of New York" (w. James W. Blake, m. Charles B. Lawlor, 1894)

"The Band Played On" (w. Charles B. Ward, m. John F. Palmer, 1895)

"When the Saints Go Marching In" (wm. anonymous, 1896)

"The Stars and Stripes Forever" (m. John Philip Sousa, 1897)

"The Victors" (wm. Louis Elbel, 1898)

"She'll Be Comin' 'Round the Mountain" (wm. anonymous, possibly 1890s)

"Maple Leaf Rag" (m. Scott Joplin, 1899)

"Go Tell It on the Mountain" (wm. anonymous late 19th or early twentieth century)

"Over the River and Through the Woods" (wm. anonymous, late 19th or early 20th century)

1900-1909

"Bill Bailey, Won't You Please Come Home?" (wm. Hughie Cannon, 1902)

"The Entertainer" (m. Scott Joplin, 1902)

"March of the Toys" (m. Victor Herbert, 1903)

"Sweet Adeline" (w. Richard H. Gerard, m. Harry Armstrong, 1903)

"Give My Regards to Broadway" (wm. George M. Cohan, 1904)

"Meet Me in St. Louis, Louis" (w. Andrew B. Sterling, m. Kerry Mills, 1904)

"Yankee Doodle Boy" (wm. George M. Cohan, 1904)

"Wait Till the Sun Shines Nellie" (w. Andrew B. Sterling, m. Harry Von Tilzer, 1905)

"National Emblem March" (m. Edwin E. Bagley, 1906)

"You're a Grand Old Flag" (wm. George M. Cohan, 1906)

"Anchors Aweigh" (wm. Alfred H. Miles, Charles A. Zimmerman, 1907)

"The Caissons Go Rolling Along" (wm. Edmund L. Gruber, 1907)

"Notre Dame Victory March" (w. John F. Shea, m. Michael J. Shea, 1908)

"Shine on Harvest Moon" (w. Jack Norworth, m., Nora Bayes Norworth, 1908)

"Take Me Out to the Ball Game" (w. Jack Norworth, m. Albert Von Tilzer, 1908)

"By the Light of the Silvery Moon" (w. Edward Madden, m. Gus Edwards, 1909)

"Casey Jones" (w. T. Lawrence Seibert, m. Eddie Newton, 1909)

"On, Wisconsin" (w. Carl Beck, m. William Thomas Purdy, 1909)

1910-1919

"Ah, Sweet Mystery of Life" (w. Rida Johnson Young, m. Victor Herbert, 1910)

"Down By the Old Mill Stream" (wm. Tell Taylor, 1910)

"Let Me Call You Sweetheart" (w. Beth Slater Whitson, m. Leo Friedman, 1910)

"Alexander's Ragtime Band" (wm. Irving Berlin, 1911)

"Oh, You Beautiful Doll" (w. A. Seymour Brown, m. Nat D. Ayer, 1911)

"Frankie and Johnny" (wm. anonymous, 1912)

"My Melancholy Baby" (w. George A. Norton, m. Ernie Burnett, 1912)

"When Irish Eyes Are Smiling" (w. Chauncy Olcott, George Graff, m. Ernest R. Ball, 1912)

"The Old Rugged Cross" (wm. George Bennard, 1913)

"You Made Me Love You" (w. Joseph McCarthy, m. James V. Monaco, 1913)

"Missouri Waltz" (w. James Royce Shannon, 1916, m. Frederic Knight Logan, 1914)

"St. Louis Blues" (wm. W. C. Handy, 1914)

"Twelfth Street Rag" (m. Euday L. Bowman, 1914)

"In the Garden" (wm. Charles Austin Miles, 1917)

"Over There" (wm. George M. Cohan, 1917)

"Sweetheart, Sweetheart, Sweetheart" (w. Rida Johnson Young, m. Sigmund Romberg, 1917)

"Tiger Rag" (wm. anonymous, 1917)

"I'm Always Chasing Rainbows" (w. Joseph McCarthy, m. Harry Carroll, 1918)

"The Marines' Hymn" (w. anonymous, 1918, m. Frenchman Jacques Offenbach, 1868)

"A Pretty Girl Is Like a Melody" (wm. Irving Berlin, 1919)

1920-1929

"Whispering" (w. Malvin Schonberger, m. John Schonberger, 1920)

"April Showers" (w. Bud DeSylva, m. Louis Silvers, 1921)

"I'm Just Wild About Harry" (wm. Noble Sissle, Eubie Blake, 1921)

"Chicago" (wm. Fred Fisher, 1922)

"Who's Sorry Now" (w. Bert Kalmar, Harry Ruby, m. Ted Snyder, 1923)

"California, Here I Come (w. Al Jolson, Bud DeSylva, m. Joseph Meyer, 1924)

"Drinking Song" (w. Dorothy Donnelly, m. Sigmund Romberg, 1924)

"Always" (wm. Irving Berlin, 1925)

"Manhattan" (w. Lorenz Hart, m. Richard Rodgers, 1925)

"Sweet Georgia Brown" (wm. Ben Bernie, Maceo Pinkard, Kenneth Casey, 1925)

"Tea for Two" (w. Irving Caesar, m. Vincent Youmans, 1925)

"The Birth of the Blues" (w. Bud DeSylva, Lew Brown, m. Ray Henderson, 1926)

"Someone to Watch Over Me" (w. Ira Gershwin, m. George Gershwin, 1926)

"The Best Things in Life Are Free" (w. Bud DeSylva, Lew Brown, m. Ray Henderson, 1927)

"I'm Looking Over a Four-Leaf Clover" (w. Mort Dixon, m. Harry Woods, 1927)

"Ol' Man River" (w. Oscar Hammerstein II, m. Jerome Kern, 1927)

"'S Wonderful" (w. Ira Gershwin, m. George Gershwin, 1927)

"Stardust" (w. Mitchell Parish, 1929, m. Hoagy Carmichael, 1927)

"Semper Paratus" (wm. Francis S. Van Boskerck, 1928)

"Ain't Misbehavin'" (w. Andy Razaf, m. Thomas "Fats" Waller, 1929)

"Happy Days Are Here Again" (w. Jack Yellen, m. Milton Ager, 1929)

"Singin' in the Rain" (w. Arthur Freed, m. Nacio Herb Brown, 1929)

1930-1939

"Embraceable You" (w. Ira Gershwin, m. George Gershwin, 1930)

"Little White Lies" (wm. Walter Donaldson, 1930)

"Strike Up the Band" (w. Ira Gershwin, m. George Gershwin, 1930)

"Of Thee I Sing" (w. Ira Gershwin, m. George Gershwin, 1931)

"Dancing in the Dark" (w. Howard Dietz, m. Arthur Schwartz, 1931)

"April in Paris" (w. Edgar Yipsel Harburg, m. Vernon Duke, 1932)

"Night and Day" (wm. Cole Porter, 1932)

"Santa Claus Is Comin' to Town" (w. Haven Gillespie, m. J. Frederick Coots, 1932)

"Easter Parade" (wm. Irving Berlin, 1933)

"Stormy Weather" (w. Ted Koehler, m. Harold Arlen, 1933)

"Deep Purple" (w. Mitchell Parish, 1939, m. Peter DeRose, 1934)

"Winter Wonderland" (w. Richard B. Smith, m. Felix Bernard, 1934)

"Begin the Beguine" (wm. Cole Porter, 1935)

"Summertime" (w. Ira Gershwin, DuBose Heyward, m. George Gershwin, 1935)

"A Fine Romance" (w. Dorothy Fields, m. Jerome Kern, 1936)

"Stompin' at the Savoy" (w. Andy Razaf, m. Benny Goodman, Edgar Sampson, Chick Webb, 1936)

"My Funny Valentine" (w. Lorenz Hart, m. Richard Rodgers, 1937)

"Sing, Sing, Sing (m. Louis Prima, 1937)

"Heart and Soul" (w. Frank Loesser, m. Hoagy Carmichael, 1938)

"The Air Force Song" (wm. Robert M. Crawford, 1939)

"God Bless America" (wm. Irving Berlin, 1939)

"Gone with the Wind Theme" (m. Max Steiner, 1939)

"In the Mood" (w. Andy Razaf, m. Joe Garland, 1939)

"Moonlight Serenade" (w. Mitchell Parish, m. Glenn Miller, 1939)

"Over the Rainbow" (w. Edgar Yipsel Harburg, m. Harold Arlen, 1939)

1940-1949

"Bewitched, Bothered, and Bewildered" (w. Lorenz Hart, m. Richard Rodgers, 1940)

"The Last Time I Saw Paris" (w. Oscar Hammerstein II, m. Jerome Kern, 1940)

"Blues in the Night" (w. Johnny Mercer, m. Harold Arlen, 1941)

"Take the A Train" (m. Billy Strayhorn, 1941)

"The White Cliffs of Dover" (w. Nat Burton, m. Walter Kent, 1941)

"White Christmas" (wm. Irving Berlin, 1942)

"Oklahoma!" (w. Oscar Hammerstein II, m. Richard Rodgers, 1943)

"Laura" (w. Johnny Mercer, m. David Raksin, 1944)

"Opus One" (m. Sy Oliver, 1944)

"Carousel Waltz" (m. Richard Rodgers, 1945)

"Let It Snow! Let It Snow! Let It Snow!" (w. Sammy Cahn, m. Jule Styne, 1945)

"We Shall Overcome" (w. anonymous, m. anonymous, possibly Roberta Evelyn Martin, 1945)

"The Christmas Song" (wm. Mel Tormé, Robert Wells, 1946)

"Show Business" (wm. Irving Berlin, 1946)

"Another Op'nin', Another Show" (wm. Cole Porter, 1948)

"Diamonds Are a Girl's Best Friend" (w. Leo Robin, m. Jule Styne, 1949)

"Dragnet Theme" (m. Walter Schumann, 1949)

"How Great Thou Art" (wm. Stuart K. Hine, 1949)

"Rudolph the Red-Nosed Reindeer" (wm. Johnny Marks, 1949)

"Some Enchanted Evening" (w. Oscar Hammerstein II, m. Richard Rodgers, 1949)

1950-1959

"Luck Be a Lady" (wm. Frank Loesser, 1950)

"I Love Lucy Theme" (w. Harold Adamson, 1953, m. Eliot Daniel, 1951)

"Silver Bells" (w. Ray Evans, m. Jay Livingston, 1951)

"The Lion Sleeps Tonight" (wm. George David Weiss, Luigi Creatore, Hugo Peretti, Albert Stanton, 1952)

"Your Cheatin' Heart" (wm. Hank Williams, 1952)

"I Love Paris" (wm. Cole Porter, 1953)

"Melancholy Serenade" (m. Jackie Gleason, 1953)

"Rock Around the Clock" (wm. Max C. Freedman, Jimmy De-Knight, 1953)

"Mack the Knife" (w. Marc Blitzstein, 1954, m. German Kurt Weill, 1928)

"Hey There" (wm. Richard Adler, Jerry Ross, 1954)

"Shake Rattle and Roll" (wm. Charles Calhoun, 1954)

"Ain't That a Shame" (wm. Antoine "Fats" Domino, David Bartholomew, 1955)

"Love and Marriage" (w. Sammy Cahn, m. Jimmy Van Heusen, 1955)

"Misty" (w. Johnny Burke, m. Erroll Garner, 1955)

"The Banana Boat Song" ("Day-O") (wm. Erik Darling, Bob Carey, Alan Arkin, 1956)

"Blue Suede Shoes" (wm. Carl Lee Perkins, 1956)

"Hound Dog" (wm. Jerry Leiber, Mike Stoller, 1956)

"Love Me Tender" (wm. Elvis Presley, Vera Matson, 1956)

"Standing on the Corner" (wm. Frank Loesser, 1956)

"Chances Are" (w. Al Stillman, m. Robert Allen, 1957)

"Jailhouse Rock" (wm. Jerry Leiber, Mike Stoller, 1957)

"Perry Mason Theme" (m. Fred Steiner, 1957)

"Seventy-Six Trombones" (wm. Meredith Willson, 1957)

"Tonight" (w. Stephen Sondheim, m. Leonard Bernstein, 1957)

"Peter Gunn Theme" (m. Henry Mancini, 1958)

"Satin Doll" (w. Johnny Mercer, m. Billy Strayhorn, Duke Ellington, 1958)

"Surfin' USA" (w. Brian Wilson, 1963, m. Chuck Berry, 1958)

"Bonanza Theme" (w. Ray Evans, m. Jay Livingston, 1959)

"High Hopes" (w. Sammy Cahn, m. Jimmy Van Heusen, 1959)

"Olympic Fanfare" (m. Leo Arnaud, 1959)

"Rawhide Theme" (w. Ned Washington, m. Dmitri Tiomkin, 1959)

"The Sound of Music" (w. Oscar Hammerstein II, m. Richard Rodgers, 1959)

1960-1971

"The Twist" (wm. Hank Ballard, 1960)

"Can't Help Falling in Love" (wm. George David Weiss, Luigi Creatore, Hugo Peretti, 1961)

"Moon River" (w. Johnny Mercer, m. Henry Mancini, 1961)

"Will You Love Me Tomorrow" (wm. Gerry Goffin, Carole King, 1961)

"I Left My Heart in San Francisco" (wm. Douglas A. Cross, George Cory, 1962)

"Diana" (wm. Paul Anka, 1963)

"Good Vibrations" (wm. Brian Wilson, Mike Love, 1963)

"Hello Dolly!" (wm. Jerry Herman, 1964)

"If I Were a Rich Man" (w. Sheldon Harnick, m. Jerry Bock, 1964)

"Oh, Pretty Woman" (wm. Roy Orbison, William Dees, 1964)

"Pink Panther Theme" (m. Henry Mancini, 1964)

"King of the Road" (wm. Roger Miller, 1965)

"Stop! In the Name of Love" (wm. Eddie Holland, Brian Holland, Lamont Dozier, 1965)

"Ballad of the Green Berets" (wm. Barry Sadler, 1966)

"Happy Together" (wm. Garry Bonner, Alan Gordon, 1966)

"I Feel Good" (wm. James Brown, 1966)

"Mission: Impossible Theme" (m. Lalo Schifrin, 1966)

"I'm a Believer" (wm. Neil Diamond, 1967)

"The 59th Street Bridge Song" ("Feelin' Groovy") (wm. Paul Simon, 1967)

"Up, Up and Away" (wm. Jim Webb, 1967)

"Classical Gas" (m. Mason Williams, 1968)

"Hawaii Five-O Theme" (m. Mort Stevens, 1968)

"Aquarius" (w. Gerome Ragni, James Rado, m. Galt MacDermot, 1968)

"My Way" (w. Paul Anka, m. Frenchman Jacques Revaux, 1969)

"Bridge Over Troubled Water" (wm. Paul Simon, 1970)

"Raindrops Keep Fallin' on My Head" (w. Hal David, m. Burt Bacharach, 1970)

"Jesus Christ, Superstar" (w. Tim Rice, m. Andrew Lloyd Webber, 1971)

All these songs, with so many modes, moods, and messages, are just a fraction of the cornucopia of American song. As Ira Gershwin declared in the 1930 classic he wrote with his brother George, "I Got Rhythm," "who can ask for anything more?"

HISTORICAL NOTES

ALABAMA

Alabama: Returning to Alabama after a European trip, Julia S. Tutwiler (1841-1916) wrote the inspirational lyrics of this song to counteract the depressed mood of the people during the Reconstruction period (1865-1877). In 1931, Edna Gockel Gussen wrote a tune for the lyrics and the combination was officially adopted as the state song that year.

The words:

Alabama, Alabama, we will aye be true to thee,
From thy Southern shores where groweth,
By the sea thy orange tree.
To thy Northern vale where floweth,
Deep and blue thy Tennessee,
Alabama, Alabama, we will aye be true to thee!

Broad the Stream whose name thou barest;
Grand thy Bigbee rolls along;
Fair thy Coosa-Tallapoosa
Bold thy Warrior, dark and strong,
Goodlier than the land that Moses
Climbed lone Nebo's Mount to see,
Alabama, Alabama, we will aye be true to thee!

From thy prairies broad and fertile,
Where thy snow-white cotton shines,
To the hills where coal and iron
Hide in thy exhausted mines,
Strong-armed miners–sturdy farmers;
Loyal hearts whate'er we be,
Alabama, Alabama, we will aye be true to thee!

[Haworth co-indexing entry note]: "Historical Notes." Co-published simultaneously in *Music Reference Services Quarterly* (The Haworth Press, Inc.) Vol. 6, No. 1/2, 1997, pp. 19-74; and: *State Songs of the United States: An Annotated Anthology* (William E. Studwell and Bruce R. Schueneman) The Haworth Press, Inc., 1997, pp. 19-74. Single or multiple copies of this article are available for a fee from The Haworth Document Delivery Service [1-800-342-9678, 9:00 a.m. - 5:00 p.m. (EST). E-mail address: getinfo@haworth.com].

From thy quarries where the marble
White as that of Paros gleams
Waiting till thy sculptor's chisel,
Wake to life thy poet's dreams;
For not only wealth of nature,
Wealth of mind hast thou to fee,
Alabama, Alabama, we will aye be true to thee!

Where the perfumed south-wind whispers,
Thy magnolia groves among,
Softer than a mother's kisses,
Sweeter than a mother's song;
Where the golden jasmine trailing,
Woos the treasure-laden bee,
Alabama, Alabama, we will aye be true to thee!

Brave and pure thy men and women,
Better this than corn and wine,
Make us worthy, God in Heaven,
Of this goodly land of thine;
Hearts as open as our doorways,
Liberal hands and spirits free,
Alabama, Alabama, we will aye be true to thee!

Little, little, can I give thee,
Alabama, mother mine;
But that little–hand, brain, spirit,
All I have and am are thine,
Take, O take the gift and giver,
Take and serve thyself with me,
Alabama, Alabama, I will aye be true to thee!

ALASKA

Alaska's Flag: The only official state song to focus upon the state's flag, this composition ends with the modest yet proud line "The simple flag of a last frontier." Set to a 1930's melody by Elinor Dusenbury, the poem by Marie Drake (1888-1963), the territory's assistant education commissioner, was first published in 1935 and officially adopted in 1955.

ARIZONA

Arizona March Song: The words of this expansive composition include exuberant lines like "Where the wide, wide world is waiting" and, in the chorus, the proclamation "Thank God, for Arizona." Published in 1916, "Arizona March Song" was the collaborative effort of lyricist Margaret Rowe Clifford and musician Maurice Blumenthal.

The words:

Come to this land of sunshine
To this land where life is young.
Where the wide, wide world is waiting,
The songs that will now be sung.
Where the golden sun is flaming
Into warm, white, shining day,
And the sons of men are blazing
Their priceless right of way. [*chorus*]

Come stand beside the rivers
Within our valleys broad.
Stand here with heads uncovered,
In the presence of our God!
While all around, about us
The brave, unconquered band,
As guardians and landmarks
The giant mountains stand. [*chorus*]

Not alone for gold and silver
Is Arizona great.
But with graves of heroes sleeping,
All the land is consecrate!
O, come and live beside us
However far ye roam

Come help us build temples
And name those temples "home." [*chorus*]

Chorus

Sing the song that's in your hearts
Sing of the great Southwest,
Thank God, for Arizona
In splendid sunshine dressed.
For thy beauty and thy grandeur,
For thy regal robes so sheen
We hail thee Arizona
Our Goddess and our queen.

ARKANSAS

Arkansas: This song by Eva Ware Barnett, and the anonymous piece "The Arkansas Traveler," were both adopted as official state songs in 1987. Barnett's composition, of uncertain date, with the lines "I'm thinking tonight of the Southland" and "Arkansas, Arkansas, I salute thee," is more in the tradition of state songs than the folkish "Traveler."

The words:

I am thinking tonight of the Southland,
Of the home of my childhood days,
Where I roamed through woods and the meadows,
By the mill and the brook that plays;
Where the roses are in bloom,
And the sweet magnolia too,
Where the jasmine is white,
And the fields are violet blue,
There's a welcome awaits her children
Who have wandered far from home. [*chorus*]

'Tis a land full of joy and of sunshine,
Rich in pearls and in diamonds rare,

Full of hope, faith and love for the stranger
Who may pass 'neath her portals fair;
There the rice fields are full,
And the cotton, corn, and hay,
There the fruits of the field bloom in winter months and May,
'Tis the land that I love,
First of all dear,
And to her let us all give cheer. [*chorus*]

Chorus

Arkansas, Arkansas, 'tis a name dear,
'Tis the place I call "Home, Sweet Home;"
Arkansas, Arkansas, I salute thee,
From thy shelter no more I'll roam.

The Arkansas Traveler: Based on the legend of the Arkansas Traveler who encountered a fiddler who repeated the same notes on his instrument over and over, this anonymous composition is probably from the first half of the 19th century. One of the better songs from the rural United States, "Traveler," along with "Arkansas," was officially adopted as a state song in 1987.

The words:

On a lonely road quite long ago
A trav'ler trod with fiddle and a bow;
While rambling thru the country rich and grand,
He quickly sensed the magic and the beauty of the land. [*refrain*]

Many years have passed, the trav'lers gay
Repeat the tune along the highway;
And ev'ry voice that sings the glad refrain
Re-echoes from the mountains to the fields of growing grain. [*refrain*]

Refrain

For the Wonder State we'll sing a song,
And lift our voices loud and long.

For the Wonder State we'll shout Hurrah!
And praise the opportunities we find in Arkansas.

CALIFORNIA

I Love You, California: Even the names of the creators of the state's official song reflect the wide variety (both natural and man made) that is so very characteristic of California. F. B. Silverwood, with a name suggesting pleasant outdoor images, wrote the lyrics to the 1913 song, while A. F. Frankenstein, with a name suggesting the bizarre in literature, wrote the music.

The words:

I love you, California, you're the greatest state of all,
I love you in the winter, summer, spring, and in the fall,
I love your fertile valleys; your dear mountains I adore,
I love your grand old ocean and I love her rugged shore. [*chorus*]

I love your redwood forests—love your fields of yellow grain,
I love your summer breezes and I love your winter rain,
I love you, land of flowers; land of honey, fruit and wine,
I love you California; you have won this heart of mine. [*chorus*]

I love your old gray Missions—love your vineyards stretching far,
I love you, California, with your Golden Gate ajar,
I love your purple sunsets, love your skies of azure blue,
I love you California; I just can't help loving you. [*chorus*]

I love you, California, you are very dear to me,
I love you, Tamalpais, and I love Yosemite,
I love you, Land of Sunshine, half your beauties are untold,
I loved you in my childhood, and I'll love you when I'm old. [*chorus*]

Chorus

Where the snow crowned Golden Sierras
Keep their watch o'er the valleys bloom,

It is there I would be in our land by the sea,
Ev'ry breeze bearing rich perfume,
It is here nature gives of her rarest,
It is Home Sweet Home to Me,
And I know when I die I shall breathe my last sigh
For my sunny California.

California, Here I Come: The unofficial song of the Golden State, "California, Here I Come," is one of the better known compositions associated with any state. It was written in 1924 by lyricists Al Jolson (1886-1950) and Bud De Sylva (1895-1950) and composer Joseph Meyer (1894-1987), and was one of the favorite repertory pieces of the great entertainer Jolson.

COLORADO

Where the Columbines Grow: Arthur J. Fynn, a prominent educator, wrote this composition in 1911 to honor the bluish-purple state flower. Soon after, in 1915, it became the official state song, but because it failed to mention the name of the state there have been several efforts to replace it.

The words:

Where the snowy peaks gleam in the moonlight, above the dark
forests of pine,
And the wild foaming waters dash onward, toward lands where the
tropic stars shine;
Where the scream of the bold mountain eagle responds to the notes
of the dove
In the purple robed West, the land that is best, the pioneer land that
we love. [*chorus*]

The bison is gone from the upland, the deer from the canyon has fled,
The home of the wolf is deserted, the antelope moans for his dead,
The war-whoop re-echoes no longer, the Indian's only a name,
And the nymphs of the grove in their loneliness rove, but the col-
umbine blooms just the same. [*chorus*]

Let the violet brighten the brookside, in the sunlight of earlier
spring,

Let the clover bedeck the green meadow, in the days when the orioles sing,

Let the goldenrod herald the autumn, but, under the mid-summer sky,

In its fair Western home, may the columbine bloom till our great mountain rivers run dry. [*chorus*]

Chorus

'Tis the land where the columbines grow,
Overlooking the plains far below,
While the cool summer breeze in the evergreen trees
Softly sings where the columbines grow.

CONNECTICUT

Yankee Doodle: Probably written by Philadelphian Francis Hopkinson (1737-1791), a signer of the Declaration of Independence, who based the melody on a British tune, or possibly entirely English, this little piece appeared in the American colonies no later than the 1760s. It was the favorite battle song of the American soldiers in the American Revolution. The earliest versions did not contain the now familiar words "pony," "feather," and "macaroni." The composition became Connecticut's official song in 1978.

The words:

Yankee Doodle went to town,
Riding on a pony,
Stuck a feather in his hat,
And called it macaroni. [*chorus*]

Chorus

Yankee Doodle keep it up,
Yankee Doodle dandy,
Mind the music and the step,
And with the girls be handy.

A good song with "Connecticut" actually in the title is "Connecticut" (1946) by the notable songwriters Hugh Martin (1914-), composer, and Ralph Blane (1914-), lyricist.

DELAWARE

Our Delaware: This composition, which became the official state song in 1925, has three verses, one for each county in Delaware. The loving, enthusiastic lyrics were by poet, journalist, and politician George B. Hynson (1862-1926), who ran unsuccessfully for governor in 1912. The music was by Will M.S. Brown.

The words:

Oh the hills of dear New Castle,
And the smiling vales between,
When the corn is all in tassel,
And the meadow lands are green;
Where the cattle crop the clover,
And its breath is in the air,
While the sun is shining over
Our beloved Delaware. [*chorus*]

Where the wheat fields break and billow,
In the peaceful land of Kent,
Where the toiler seeks his pillow,
With the blessings of content;
Where the bloom that tints the peaches,
Cheeks of merry maidens share,
And the woodland chorus preaches
A rejoicing Delaware. [*chorus*]

Dear old Sussex visions linger,
Of the holly and the pine,
Of Henlopens Jeweled finger,
Flashing out across the brine;
Of the gardens and the hedges,
And the welcome waiting there,

For the loyal son that pledges
Faith to good old Delaware. [*chorus*]

Chorus

Oh, our Delaware! Our beloved Delaware!
For the sun is shining over our beloved Delaware,
Oh! our Delaware! our beloved Delaware!
Here's the loyal son that pledges,
Faith to good old Delaware.

FLORIDA

Old Folks at Home: Also known as "Swanee River," "Old Folks at Home" (1851) is one of the most famous compositions of the great Stephen Foster (1826-1864). It was entirely an accident that the song was named after the Suwanee River in Florida, for Foster's brother casually suggested "Suwanee" as a song title after scanning a globe. The original lyrics of this official state song were altered by the State of Florida in 1978, replacing the word "darkies" with the phrase "dear ones."

The words, with the above-mentioned change:

Way down upon the Swanee River,
Far, far, away,
There's where my heart is turning ever,
There's where the old folks stay.
All up and down the whole creation,
Sadly I roam,
Still longing for the old plantation,
And for the old folks at home. [*chorus*]

All round the little farm I wandered
When I was young,
Then many happy days I squandered,
Many the songs I sung.

When I was playing with my brother
Happy was I.
Oh! Take me to my kind old mother,
There let me live and die. [*chorus*]

One little hut among the bushes,
One that I love,
Still sadly to my mem'ry rushes,
No matter where I rove.
When will I see the bees a-humming
All around the comb?
When will I hear the banjo thumming
Down in my good old home? [*chorus*]

Chorus

All the world is sad and dreary,
Everywhere I roam,
Oh! dear ones how my heart grows weary,
Far from the old folks at home.

GEORGIA

Georgia: Georgia has had two official state songs. While "Georgia on My Mind," the current state song, is much better known, "Georgia" was declared the first official state song by the Georgia Legislature in 1958. More traditional and less intense than the current state song, undated "Georgia" features lyrics by Robert Loveman and music by Lollie Belle Wylie.

The words:

From the mountains to the sea,
Where her rivers roll,
There I long to be,
O, my heart; my soul;
By her meadows let me lie,

In her vales remain,
Underneath her rooftree sky
Watch the seasons wane.

Georgia land of our delight,
Haven of the blest,
Here by happy day and night,
Peace enthrones the breast;
Georgia, Georgia dearest earth,
Underneath the blue,
Clime that ever giveth birth
To the brave and true.

Georgia on My Mind: Though very good, the official state song "Georgia on My Mind" (1930) was definitely not the most famous composition by musician Hoagy Carmichael (1899-1981). Carmichael also wrote the 1927 mini-masterpiece "Stardust," one of the most beloved popular songs of the 20th century, plus several other standards. Stuart Gorrell, who wrote the words for "Georgia on My Mind," also reportedly gave "Stardust" its name.

HAWAII

Hawai'i Pono'i: Formerly Hawaii's national anthem and since 1967 its state song, the words for "Hawai'i Pono'i" were written by David Kalakaua in 1874. Henry Berger composed the music shortly afterwards, which has some resemblance to "God Save the King." Today, *Hawai'i Aloha,* by Lorenzo Lyons (1807-1886), is often performed in place of Kalakaua's piece.

The words:

Hawaii's own true sons
Be loyal to your chief
Your country's liege and lord, the Ali'i. [*chorus*]

Hawaii's own true sons
Honor give to your chiefs

Of kindred race are we,
Younger descent. [*chorus*]

Hawaii's own true sons,
People of this our land;
Duty calls fealty,
Guide in the right. [*chorus*]

Chorus

Father above us all,
Kamehameha,
Who guarded us from war
With his ihe.

IDAHO

Here We Have Idaho: Idaho has only one official state song, but there are two versions of it, both of uncertain date. The full song, with music by Sallie Hume-Douglas, words for the verses by Albert J. Tompkins, and words for the chorus by McKinley Helm (1896-), is the official version. However, sometimes only the chorus is printed.

The words:

You've heard of the wonders our land does possess,
It's beautiful valleys and hills,
The majestic forests where nature abounds,
We love every nook and rill. [*chorus*]

There's truly one state in this great land of ours
Where ideals can be realized.
The pioneers made it so for you and me,
A legacy we'll always prize. [*chorus*]

Chorus

And here we have Idaho
Winning her way to fame

Silver and gold in the sunlight blaze,
And romance lies in her name.
Singing, we're singing of you
Ah, proudly too,
All our lives through, we'll go
Singing, singing of you,
Singing of Idaho.

ILLINOIS

Illinois: This official state song of the "Land of Lincoln," adopted in 1925, does not fail to mention Lincoln (in the 4th verse). But the now somewhat antiquated 1893 verses by Charles H. Chamberlin also refer to the rivers, prairies, and other features of the state. The melody, originally composed for the 1875 popular song "Baby Mine," is by Archibald Johnston.

The words:

By thy rivers gently flowing, Illinois, Illinois,
O'er thy prairies verdant growing, Illinois, Illinois,
Comes an echo on the breeze,
Rustling through the leafy trees, and its mellow tones are these,
Illinois, Illinois,
And its mellow tones are these, Illinois, Illinois.

From a wilderness of prairies, Illinois, Illinois,
Straight thy way and never varies, Illinois, Illinois,
Till upon the inland sea,
Stands thy great commercial tree, turning all the world to thee,
Illinois, Illionois,
Turning all the world to thee, Illinois.

When you heard your country calling, Illinois, Illinois,
Where the shot and shell were falling, Illinois, Illinois,
When the Southern host withdrew,
Pitting Gray against the Blue, there were none more brave than you,
Illinois, Illinois,
There were none more brave than you, Illinois, Illinois.

Not without thy wondrous story, Illinois, Illinois,
Can be writ the nation's glory, Illinois, Illinois,
On the record of thy years,
Abraham Lincoln's name appears, Grant and Logan, and our tears,
Illinois, Illinois,
Grant and Logan, and our tears, Illinois.

INDIANA

Indiana or *Back Home Again in Indiana* or *My Indiana Home*:
This favorite song is sometimes thought to be the state's official
song. The 1917 composition was by lyricist Ballard MacDonald
(1882-1935) and composer James F. Hanley (1892-1942). The
song is part of the ceremonies of the annual Indianapolis 500
race.

The words:

I have always been a wand'rer, over land and sea,
Yet a moonbeam on the water casts a spell o'er me,
A vision fair I see, again I seem to be. [*chorus*]

Fancy paints on mem'ry's canvas scenes that we hold dear,
We recall them in days after, clearly they appear,
And often times I see a scene that's dear to me. [*chorus*]

Chorus

Back home again in Indiana, and it seems that I can see
The gleaming candle light still shining bright through the syca-
    mores for me,
The new mown hay sends all its fragrance from the fields I used to
    roam,
When I dream about the moonlight on the Wabash, then I long for
    my Indiana home.

On the Banks of the Wabash, Far Away: Paul Dresser (1858-1906), a brother of the famous novelist Theodore Drieser, wrote the words and music for Indiana's official state song in 1897. Nostalgic, sweet, and sentimental, the ballad became a national favorite. Just one of a body of fine Indiana songs, it became the state's song in 1913.

The words:

Round my Indiana homestead wave the cornfield,
In the distance loom the woodlands clear and cool.
Often times my thoughts revert to scenes of childhood,
Where I first received my lessons, nature's school.
But one thing there is missing in the picture,
Without her face it seems so incomplete.
I long to see mother in the doorway,
As she stood there years ago, her boy to greet!

Many years have passed since I strolled by the river,
Arm in arm with sweet Mary by my side.
It was there I tried to tell her that I loved her,
It was there I begged of her to be my bride.
Long years have passed since I strolled thro' the churchyard.
She's sleeping there my angel Mary, dear.
I loved her but she thought I didn't mean it,
Still I'd give my future were she only here.

Refrain

Oh, the moonlight's fair tonight along the Wabash,
From the fields there comes the breath of new mown hay.
Thro' the sycamores the candle lights are gleaming,
On the banks of the Wabash, far away.

IOWA

Iowa Corn Song: Although not the official state song, the "Iowa Corn Song," with its unique line "Ioway, that's where the tall corn grows" is perhaps Iowa's best known song. The first verse of the lyrics was penned by George Hamilton in 1912. With added lyrics by Ray W. Lockard, and set to a tune by Edward Riley, the composition was published in 1921.

The words:

Let's sing of Grand old Ioway,
Yo-ho, yo-ho, yo-ho,
Our love is stronger ev'ry day,
Yo-ho, yo-ho, yo-ho.
So come along and join the throng,
Sev'ral hundred thousand strong,
As you come just sing this song,
Yo-ho, yo-ho, yo-ho. [*chorus*]

Our land is full of ripening corn,
Yo-ho, yo-ho, yo-ho,
We've watched it grow both night and morn,
Yo-ho, yo-ho, yo-ho.
But now we rest, we've stood the test,
All that's good we have the best,
Ioway has reached the crest,
Yo-ho, yo-ho, yo-ho. [*chorus*]

Chorus

Ioway, Ioway,
State of all the land,
Joy on ev'ry hand.
We're from Ioway, Ioway.
That's where the tall corn grows.

The Song of Iowa: The words for this official state song were created in 1897 by Samuel Hawkins Marshall Byers (1838-1933). The music was the tune used for the possibly 16th or 17th century German carol "O Tannenbaum" and also for another state song, "Maryland, My Maryland." Despite this song's official status, another state song, "Iowa Corn Song," is more famous.

The words:

You ask what land I love the best, Iowa, 'tis Iowa,
The fairest State of all the west, Iowa, O! Iowa,
From yonder Mississippi's stream
To where Missouri's waters gleam
O! fair it is as poet's dream, Iowa, in Iowa.

See yonder fields of tasselled corn, Iowa, in Iowa,
Where plenty fills her golden horn, Iowa, in Iowa,
See how her wondrous prairies shine
To yonder sunset's purpling line,
O! happy land, O! land of mine, Iowa, O! Iowa.

And she has maids whose laughing eyes, Iowa, O! Iowa,
To him who loves were Paradise, Iowa, O! Iowa,
O! happiest fate that e'er was known.
Such eyes to shine for one alone,
To call such beauty all his own, Iowa, O! Iowa.

Go read the story of thy past, Iowa, O! Iowa,
What glorious deeds, what fame thou hast! Iowa, Iowa,
So long as time's great cycle runs,
Or nations weep their fallen ones,
Thou'lt not forget thy patriot sons, Iowa, O! Iowa.

KANSAS

Home on the Range: This official song is the stereotypical cowboy composition, and has even been called "the cowboy's national anthem." The words were probably by pioneer physician Brewster M. Higley (1823-1911) and the music was probably by musician and entertainer Daniel E. Kelley (1843-1905). The 1873 words were joined with the melody when the music was first published in 1904.

The words:

O give me a home, where the buffalo roam
Where the deer and the antelope play,

Where seldom is heard a discouraging word
And the skies are not cloudy all day. [*chorus*]

Where the air is so pure, the zephyrs so free,
The breezes so balmy and light,
That I would not exchange my home on the range
For all the cities so bright. [*chorus*]

Oh, give me a land where the bright diamond sand
Flows leisurely down the stream;
Where the graceful white swan goes gliding along
Like a maid in a heavenly dream. [*chorus*]

The red man was pressed from this part of the West,
He's likely no more to return
To the banks of Red River where seldom if ever
Their flickering campfires burn. [*chorus*]

How often at night when the heavens are bright
With the light of the glittering stars,
Have I stood here amazed and asked as I gazed
If their glory exceeds that of ours. [*chorus*]

Oh, I love these wild flowers in this dear land of ours;
The curlew I love to hear scream;
And I love the white rocks and the antelope flocks
That graze on the mountain-tops green. [*chorus*]

Then I would not exchange my home on the range,
Where the deer and the antelope play;
Where seldom is heard a discouraging word
And the skies are not cloudy all day. [*chorus*]

Chorus

Home, home on the range,
Where the deer and the antelope play,
Where seldom is heard a discouraging word
And the skies are not cloudy all day.

KENTUCKY

My Old Kentucky Home, Good Night: There is a legend that the inspiration for this 1853 hymn-like song came from an unverified 1852 trip to Kentucky by northerner Stephen Foster (1826-1864). More likely, Foster was inspired by Harriet Beecher Stowe's 1851 classic *Uncle Tom's Cabin*. The song is also the theme for the annual Kentucky Derby. As far as is known, the word "darkies" in this official state song has not been officially replaced.

The words, with "darkies" altered to "people":

The sun shines bright in the old Kentucky home,
'Tis summer, the people are gay;
The corntop's ripe and the meadow's in bloom,
While the birds make music all the day;
The young folks roll on the little cabin floor,
All merry, all happy and bright,
By'n by hard times comes a-knocking at the door,
Then my old Kentucky home, good-night! [*chorus*]

They hunt no more for the 'possum and the coon,
On the meadow, the hill, and the shore,
They sing no more by the glimmer of the moon,
On the bench by the old cabin door;
The day goes by like a shadow o'er the heart,
With sorrow, where all was delight;
The time has come when the people have to part,
Then my old Kentucky home, good-night! [*chorus*]

The head must bow and the back will have to bend,
Wherever the people may go;
A few more days and the trouble all will end
In the field where the sugarcane grow;
A few more days for to tote the weary load,
No matter, 'twill never be light,
A few more days till we totter on the road,
Then my old Kentucky home, good-night! [*chorus*]

Chorus

Weep no more my lady, O weep no more today!
We will sing one song for the old Kentucky home,
For the old Kentucky home far away.

LOUISIANA

Give Me Louisiana: The official song of the Pelican State, the Bayou State, the Sugar State, and the Creole State, "Give Me Louisiana" directly or indirectly touches upon all these nicknames. It was written by Doralice Fontane in 1970. Another state song is the 1940 country/western standard "You Are My Sunshine," by Jimmie Davis and Charles Mitchell. Another song about Louisiana is "Louisiana" (1920), words by Arthur Freed (1894-1973), music by Oliver G. Wallace (1887-1963), both popular songwriters of note.

My Louisiana: The composer of this song was a New Orleans native, Henry W. Wehrman, Jr. (1871-1956). A virtuoso violinist, he also served as organist in several churches in New Orleans and taught at Louisiana State University. "My Louisiana" (1912), with words by Howard A. Winburn, was dedicated to the Louisiana Historical Society.

The words:

Down in the ever glades
Bayous and cooling shades
Flowers and sweetest maids
All so divine.
Birds sing their sweetest songs
That's where my heart belongs
For dear old Dixie land my heart does pine. [*refrain*]

Land where the mellow moon
Shines on the old lagoon
Where sweet magnolias bloom
And dreams come true.

Rice fields and sugar cane
Song birds and golden grain
Nature's own grand domain when skies are blue. [*refrain*]

Refrain

My Louisiana, dear Louisiana
Down where the roses forever bloom.
And in the Springtime, the glorious Maytime
I'm going back to Louisiana, that's my home, sweet home.

MAINE

State of Maine: Also known under the more picturesque title "O Pine Tree State," this good song is quite descriptive of the many natural assets of the state. Written by Portland born lawyer Roger Vinton Snow (1890-1952), it was selected as the best of 115 compositions in a 1931 contest. In 1937, it became the official song of Maine.

The words:

Grand State of Maine, proudly we sing
To tell your glories to the land
To shout your praises till the echoes ring
Should fate unkind send us to roam
The scent of fragrant pines,
The tang of the salty sea will call us home. [*chorus*]

Chorus

Oh Pine Tree State
Your woods, fields and hills
Your lakes, streams and rockbound coast
Will ever fill our hearts with thrills
And though we seek far and wide
Our search will be in vain

To find a fairer spot on earth
Than Maine! Maine! Maine!

MARYLAND

Maryland, My Maryland!: The stately tune, first used for the possibly 16th or 17th century German carol "O Tannenbaum," makes this state song one of the most familiar. The fervent words, which were written around the beginning of the U.S. Civil War (1861) by Confederate sympathizer James Ryder Randall (1839-1908), seem out of place today.

The words:

The despot's heel is on thy shore,
Maryland, My Maryland!
His touch is at thy temple door,
Maryland, My Maryland!
Avenge the patriotic gore
That fleck'd the streets of Baltimore,
And be the Battle Queen of yore,
Maryland, My Maryland!

Hark to a wand'ring Son's appeal,
Maryland, My Maryland!
My Mother State! to thee I kneel,
Maryland, My Maryland!
For life and death, for woe and weal,
Thy peerless chivalry reveal,
And gird thy beauteous limbs with steel,
Maryland, My Maryland!

Thou wilt not cower in the dust,
Maryland, My Maryland!
Thy beaming sword shall never rust,
Maryland, My Maryland!
Remember Carroll's sacred trust,
Remember Howard's warlike thrust–

And all thy slumberers with the just,
Maryland, My Maryland!

Come! for thy shield is bright and strong,
Maryland, My Maryland!
Come! For thy dalliance does thee wrong,
Maryland, My Maryland!
Come! to thine own heroic throng,
That stalks with Liberty along,
And give a new Key to thy song,
Maryland, My Maryland!

Dear Mother! burst the tyrant's chain,
Maryland, My Maryland!
Virginia should not call in vain!
Maryland, My Maryland!
She meets her sisters on the plain—
"Sic semper" tis the proud refrain,
That baffles minions back amain,
Maryland, My Maryland!

I see the blush upon the cheek,
Maryland, My Maryland!
But thou wast ever bravely meek,
Maryland, My Maryland!
But lo! There surges forth a shriek
From hill to hill, from creek to creek—
Potomac calls to Chesapeake,
Maryland, My Maryland!

Thou wilt not yield the vandal toll,
Maryland, My Maryland!
Thou wilt not crook to his control,
Maryland, My Maryland!
Better the fire upon the roll,
Better the blade, the shot, the bowl,
Than crucifixion of the soul,
Maryland, My Maryland!

I hear the distant thunder-hum,
Maryland, My Maryland!
The Old Line's bugle, fife and drum,
Maryland, My Maryland!
She is not dead, nor deaf, nor dumb—
Huzza! she spurns the Northern scum!
She breathes—she burns! she'll come! she'll come!
Maryland, My Maryland!

MASSACHUSETTS

All Hail to Massachusetts: Arthur J. Marsh of Wellesley died shortly before the legislature officially designated his composition, "All Hail to Massachusetts," the official state song in 1966. Arlo Guthrie's "Massachusetts" is the state's folk song. Another song about Massachusetts is "Massachusetts" (1942), words by Andy Razaf (1895-1973), music by Luckey Roberts (1887-1968), both popular songwriters.

The words:

All hail to Massachusetts, the land of the free and the brave!
For Bunker Hill and Charlestown, and flag we love to wave,
For Lexington and Concord, and the shot heard round the world,
All hail to Massachusetts, we'll keep her flag unfurled.
She stands upright for freedom's light that shines from sea to sea,
All hail to Massachusetts! Our country 'tis of thee!

All hail to grand old Bay State, the home of the bean and the cod!
Where pilgrims found a landing and gave their thanks to God.
A land for opportunity in the good old USA,
Where men live long and prosper, and people come to stay.
Don't sell her short but learn to court her in industry and stride,
All hail the grand old Bay State! The land of pilgrim's pride!

All hail to Massachusetts, renowned in the Hall of Fame!
How proudly wave her banners emblazoned with her name!
In unity and brotherhood, sons and daughters go hand in hand,

All hail to Massachusetts, there is no finer land!
It's Massachusetts.
All hail to Massachusetts! All hail! All hail! All hail!

MICHIGAN

My Michigan: Michigan has no official state song, but there are several song titles containing the words "My Michigan." In addition to "My Michigan," published in 1910 by Oliver D. Salisbury, there is "My Michigan" by Giles Kavanaugh and H. O'Reilly Clint, "My Michigan" by Orien Dalley, and "Michigan, My Michigan" by William Otto Miessner and Douglas Malloch. A commercially successful song about Michigan by a well-known composer is "I Want to Go Back to Michigan" (1914) by the great Irving Berlin (1888-1989).

The words, with "darkies" altered to "people:":

I have wandered down in sunny Mississippi,
Where the sugarcane and cotton blossomes grow.
I have heard the people sing in Alabama
And made love to dusky maids in Idaho.
But there's just one spot that holds affection,
With its murm'ring pines beside the inland sea,
In Michigan, my Michigan, the only land in all the world for me.
[*chorus*]

Some day when fortune smiles down on me,
And the labor of the day is done,
Back to the land I love,
I'll wander back to the hills where for me life begun.
And I'll rest and dream of one who's gone and left me,
Till the time when I may join her, bye and bye.
In Michigan, my Michigan, she's sweetly sleeping 'neath thy azure
    sky. [*chorus*]

Chorus

Softly the twilight is falling
Over the crystal seas,

Gently the breezes are whisp'ring
In the sweetscented trees.
Back to my boyhood I wander,
My sweetheart is waiting once more
By the moss covered pine in the dooryard,
Down by old Michigan's shore.

Michigan, My Michigan: Since Michigan has neither an official state song nor a well-known unofficial composition, two somewhat different pieces of similar age and with similar titles are mentioned in this collection. This one, published in 1911, was a collaboration of musician William Otto Miessner (1880-1967) and lyricist Douglas Malloch.

The words:

A song to thee, fair State of mine,
Michigan, my Michigan;
But greater song than this is thine,
Michigan, my Michigan;
The whisper of the forest tree,
The thunder of the inland sea,
Unite in one grand symphony
Of Michigan, my Michigan.

I sing a State of all the best,
Michigan, my Michigan;
I sing a State with riches blest,
Michigan, my Michigan;
Thy mines unmask a hidden store,
But richer thy historic lore,
More great the love thy builders bore,
Oh, Michigan, my Michigan.

How fair the bosom of thy lakes,
Michigan, my Michigan;
What melody each river makes,
Michigan, my Michigan;
As to thy lakes thy rivers tend,

Thy exiled children to thee send
Devotion that shall never end,
Oh, Michigan, my Michigan.

Thou rich in wealth that makes a State,
Michigan, my Michigan;
Thou great in things that make us great,
Michigan, my Michigan;
Our loyal voices sound thy claim
Upon the golden roll of Fame
Our loyal hands shall write the name
Of Michigan, my Michigan.

MINNESOTA

Hail! Minnesota: In 1904, a play based on a 1903 football game between Michigan and Minnesota was presented at the University of Minnesota. Part of the production was a new song, "Hail! Minnesota," with music and two verses by Truman E. Rickard. A verse by Arthur E. Upson later replaced Rickard's second verse, and the joint composition became official in 1945.

The words:

Minnesota Hail to thee!
Hail to thee our state so dear,
Thy light shall ever be
A beacon bright and clear.
Thy sons and daughters true
Will proclaim thee near and far,
They will guard thy fame and adore thy name;
Thou shalt be their Northern Star.

Like the stream that bends to sea,
Like the pine that seeks the blue;
Minnesota, still for thee
Thy sons are strong and true.
From thy woods and waters fair;

From thy prairies waving far,
At thy call they throng with their shout and song;
Hailing thee their Northern Star.

MISSISSIPPI

Go, Mississippi: Highlighted by the spelling out of "Mississippi" at the end of the chorus, "Go Mississippi" by Houston Davis is a well crafted and distinctive composition of uncertain date. A committee formed by the Jackson Board of Realtors in 1962 to select a state song chose "Go, Mississippi" and the legislature officially gave their approval later that year.

Mississippi Days: This 1916 song features lyrics by Ballard MacDonald (1882-1935), who also wrote songs honoring Ohio ("Beautiful Ohio") and Indiana ("Indiana"). The music was penned by Al Piantadosi (1884-1955). Piantadosi wrote several well known songs, including "I'm Awfully Glad I'm Irish" (1910), "That's How I Need You" (1912), and "The Curse of an Aching Heart" (1913). His 1915 "I Didn't Raise My Boy to Be a Soldier" expressed the anti-war sentiment of the time.

The words:

Watermelons never grew on huckleberry vines,
You won't find a snow bird nesting in the Southern climes,
Where things grow they ought to be,
Take them some place else and see,
They'll fade away and pine and die,
And that's what's wrong with me: [*chorus*]

Pick a rose and put it on the parlor mantle shelf,
It will only droop and die, the same case fits myself,
When I can't see friends I know,
Places that my heart loves so,
I'm like the rose that never grows
'Cept where it's s'posed to grow: [*chorus*]

Chorus

Those Mississippi days,
And Mississippi ways,

Those old plantation songs,
While steamboats puffed, puffed along, puffed along up the river,
Mississippi nights,
And Mississippi sights,
Oh! How my heart is burning,
Thoughts are turning,
I'm yearning,
How I miss those Mississippi days.

MISSOURI

Missouri Waltz: In 1914, Frederic Knight Logan (1871-1928) created this charming melody, quite probably borrowing from an anonymous black composer. (John Valentine Eppel is sometimes mentioned as the composer or discoverer of the music.) Two years later James Royce (1881-1946), using the pseudonym James Royce Shannon, wrote the lyrics. In addition to being a top hit of its time and one of the finest official state songs, the piece was also the unofficial theme of Harry Truman's administration.

The words, with "pickaninies" replaced by "old folks" and "mammy" replaced by "Mommy":

Hush a-bye, ma baby, slumber time is comin' soon;
Rest yo' head upon my breast while Mommy hums a tune;
The sandman is callin' where shadows are fallin',
While the soft breezes sigh as in days long gone by.

Way down in Missouri where I heard this melody,
When I was a little child on my Mommy's knee;
The old folks were hummin', their banjos were strummin'
So sweet and low.

Strum, strum, strum, strum, strum,
Seems I hear those banjos playin' once again,
Hum, hum, hum, hum, hum,
That same old plaintive strain.

Hear that mournful melody,
It just haunts you the whole day long,
And you wander in dreams back to Dixie, it seems,
When you hear that old time song.
Hush a-bye, ma baby, go to sleep on Mommy's knee,
Journey back to Dixieland in dreams again with me;
It seems like your Mommy is there again,
And the old folks were strummin' that same old refrain.

'Way down in Missouri where I learned this lullaby,
When the stars were blinkin' and the moon was climbin' high,
Seems I hear voices low, as in days long ago
Singin' hush a-bye.

MONTANA

Montana Melody: In 1981 LeGrand Harvey and Carleen Harvey of Missoula wrote this song which expressively describes the natural wonders of the state. In 1983, the state legislature was asked to make "Montana Melody" the official state song, but instead the legislators, not wishing to replace the official song "Montana," compromised by naming "Montana Melody" as the state ballad.

Montana: Joseph E. Howard (1878-1961), a successful composer who also wrote the tunes for "I Wonder Who's Kissing Her Now" (1909) and "Hello, Ma Baby" (1899), was touring Butte in 1910. On the suggestion of a local resident, Howard wrote a melody and Charles C. Cohan, a Butte journalist, supplied some lyrics. The resulting song became official in 1945.

The words:

Tell me of that Treasure State
Story always new,
Tell of its beauties grand
And its hearts so true.
Mountains of sunset fire
The land I love the best.

Let me grasp the hand of one
From out the golden West. [*refrain*]

Each country has its flow'r;
Each one plays a part,
Each bloom brings a longing hope
To some lonely heart,
Bitter Root to me is dear
Growing in my land.
Sing then that glorious air
The one I understand. [*refrain*]

Refrain

Montana, Montana,
Glory of the West,
Of all the states from coast to coast,
You're easily the best.
Montana, Montana,
Where skies are always blue,
Montana, Montana,
I love you.

NEBRASKA

Beautiful Nebraska: Jim Fras, a Russian emigré and professional entertainer who came to Lincoln in 1952, wrote the music for this 1965 song and collaborated on the words with Guy G. Miller. With several repetitions of the phrase "Beautiful Nebraska," it had no trouble becoming the official state song in 1967.

The words:

Beautiful Nebraska, peaceful prairie land,
Laced with many rivers and the hills of sand;
Dark green valleys cradled in the earth,
Rain and sunshine bring abundant birth.

Beautiful Nebraska, as you look around,
You will find a rainbow reaching the ground;
All these wonders by the Master's hand;
Beautiful Nebraska land.

We are so proud of this state where we live,
There is no place that has so much to give.

Beautiful Nebraska, as you look around,
You will find a rainbow reaching the ground;
All these wonders by the Master's hand;
Beautiful Nebraska land.

NEVADA

Home Means Nevada: Written in 1932 by Bertha Raffetto of Reno
in an all night composition session, this bouncy march became an
overnight hit after Raffetto sang it at a Nevada Day celebration. It
became official the next year. Some years later the song gained
some national exposure at three consecutive Republican conven-
tions when it accompanied presidential nominating speeches by a
Nevada senator.

NEW HAMPSHIRE

New Hampshire, My New Hampshire: In 1947, New Hampshire
declared nine compositions to be state songs. The second on the list
was "New Hampshire, My New Hampshire," a composition of
unknown date, with words by Julius Richelson and music by Walter
P. Smith. Thirty years later, the legislature made the first song on the
1947 list, "Old New Hampshire," the official state song.

The words:

From the top of old New England,
To the shores of Portsmouth Bay,

A land known as the Granite State
With its lakes and mountains lay,
From lofty mountain splendor to enchanting vales below,
God's glory is reflected in the homeland that we know.

Old New Hampshire: Created in 1926 by lyricist John F. Holmes and composer Maurice Hoffmann, both of Manchester, "Old New Hampshire" was just the first composition on a 1947 list of nine state songs until selected as the only official state song by the legislature in 1977.

The words:

With a skill that knows no measure,
From the golden store of Fate,
God, in His great love and wisdom,
Made the rugged Granite State;
Made the lakes, the fields, the forests;
Made the rivers and the rills;
Made the bubbling, crystal fountains
Of New Hampshire's Granite Hills. [*refrain*]

Builded He New Hampshire glorious
From the borders to the sea;
And with matchless charm and splendor
Blessed her for eternity.
Here, the majesty of mountains;
Here, the grandeur of the lake;
Here, the truth as from the hillside
Whence her crystal waters break. [*refrain*]

Refrain

Old New Hampshire, Old New Hampshire,
Old New Hampshire grand and great,
We will sing of Old New Hampshire,
Of the dear old Granite State.

NEW JERSEY

Ode to New Jersey: New Jersey has no official song. However, the anonymous and undated "Ode to New Jersey" would be a good candidate. It has an excellent tune derived from the possibly 16th or 17th century German Carol "O Tannenbaum" and which is also used for the state songs "Song of Iowa" and "Maryland, My Maryland." It also has a good title and inspirational opening lines. Another song honoring New Jersey is Frank L. Ryerson's "Tercentenary March" (1964), written to celebrate the state's 300th anniversary.

The words:

The rolling wave is on thy shore,
Jerseyland, my Jerseyland!
Aloft thine azure mountains soar,
Jerseyland, my Jerseyland!
Hilltop and vale, lowly lying plain,
Thy pines, thy streams with murm'ring strain,
These ne'er will let thy beauty wane,
Jerseyland, my Jerseyland!

NEW MEXICO

O, Fair New Mexico: Officially adopted in 1917, this passionate state song of uncertain date was created by Elizabeth Garrett, the blind daughter of the famous lawman Pat Garrett. John Philip Sousa made an arrangement of in it 1928. A second composition, the Spanish language "Así es Nuevo México," by Amadeo Lucero, was also officially adopted as a state song in 1971.

The words:

Under a sky of azure,
Where the balmy breezes blow;
Kissed by the golden sunshine,
Is Nuevo Mejico.
Home of Montezuma,
With fiery heart aglow,
State of the deeds historic,
Is Nuevo Mejico. [*chorus*]

Rugged and high sierras,
With deep canyons below;
Dotted with fertile valleys,
Is Nuevo Mejico.
Fields full of sweet alfalfa,
Richest perfumes bestow,
State of apple blossoms,
Is Nuevo Mejico. [*chorus*]

Days that are full of heart-dreams,
Nights when the moon hangs low;
Beaming its benediction,
O'er Nuevo Mejico.
Land with its bright manana,
Coming through weal and woe;
State of our esperanza,
Is Nuevo Mejico. [*chorus*]

Chorus

O, fair New Mexico,
We love, we love you so,
Our hearts with pride o'erflow,
No matter where we go,
O, fair New Mexico,
We love, we love you so,
The grandest state to know,
New Mexico.

Asi Es Neuvo México: Reflecting the bilingual nature of the Southwestern United States, New Mexico officially adopted this fine Spanish language composition soon after it was written in 1971. Created by Amadeo Lucero, who died in 1987, it shares the honor of being the state's song with Elizabeth Garrett's "O, Fair New Mexico."

NEW YORK

The Sidewalks of New York: Much music has been composed in New York State, yet there is no official state song. Probably the best

known song about New York is the charming 1894 ballad "The
Sidewalks of New York." In the true melting pot tradition of the
city, New York native James W. Blake (1862-1935) collaborated
with Irish immigrant Charles B. Lawlor (1852-1925).

The words:

Down in front of Casey's,
Old brown wooden stoop,
On a summer's evening,
We formed a merry group;
Boys and girls together,
We would sing and waltz,
While the "Ginnie" played the organ
On the sidewalks of New York. [*chorus*]

That's where Johnny Casey,
And little Jimmy Crowe,
With Jackey Krause the baker,
Who always had the dough,
Pretty Nellie Shannon,
With a dude as light as cork,
First picked up the waltz step
On the sidewalks of New York. [*chorus*]

Things have changed since those times,
Some are up in "G,"
Others they are on the hog,
But they all feel just like me,
They would part with all they've got
Could they but once more walk,
With their best girl and have a twirl,
On the sidewalks of New York. [*chorus*]

Chorus

East side, West side, all around the town,
The tots play "Ring-a-rosie,"
"London Bridge is falling down!"

Boys and girls together,
Me and Mamie Rorke,
Tripped the light fantastic
On the sidewalks of New York.

New York, Our Empire State: New York has no official song but has a famous ballad, "The Sidewalks of New York," included in this collection. "Sidewalks," however, is only about New York City. To give representation to the remainder of this large and complex state, a second song is mentioned: "New York, Our Empire State," by composer Etta H. Morris and lyricist Caroline Fitzsimmons. It is uncertain when this composition was written.

NORTH CAROLINA

The Old North State: In 1835, William Gaston (1778-1844), a lawyer, legislator, congressman, jurist, and staunch supporter of religious freedom, wrote the lyrics for "The Old North State." About that time, an Austrian troupe which visited Raleigh used a Hungarian song in their performance, and from that song a tune for Gaston's words was derived. The song became official in 1927.

The words:

Carolina! Carolina! Heaven's blessings attend her!
While we live we will cherish, protect and defend her;
Though the scorner may sneer at and witlings defame her,
Our hearts swell with gladness whenever we name her. [*chorus*]

Though she envies not others their merited glory,
Say, whose name stands foremost in Liberty's story!
Though too true to herself e'er to crouch to oppression,
Who can yield to just rule more loyal submission? [*chorus*]

Plain and artless her sons, but whose doors open faster
At the knock of a stranger, or the tale of disaster?
How like to the rudeness of their dear native mountains,
With rich ore in their bosoms and life in their fountains. [*chorus*]

And her daughters, the Queen or the Forest resembling—
So graceful, so constant, yet to gentlest breath trembling,
And true lightwood at heart, let the match be applied them,
How they kindle and flame! Oh! none know but who've tried them.
[*chorus*]

Then let all who love us, love the land we live in
(As happy a region on this side of Heaven),
Where Plenty and Freedom, Love and Peace smile before us,
Raise aloud, raise together, the heart-thrilling chorus! [*chorus*]

Chorus

Hurrah! Hurrah! The Old North State forever!
Hurrah! Hurrah! The good Old North State!

NORTH DAKOTA

North Dakota Hymn: In addition to this official state song written in 1927 by composer Clarence Simeon Putnam (1859-1944) of Fargo and lyricist James William Foley (1874-1939), other North Dakota songs include "North Dakota" by Hjalmer A. Swenson and "The Flickertail," a march by James D. Ployhar. Flickertails are native ground squirrels that are the source of the nickname "The Flicker-tail State."

OHIO

Beautiful Ohio: Ballard MacDonald (1882-1935) not only wrote the lyrics for this excellent official state song but also the words for another even better known though unofficial state song, "Indiana." The composer of the melody for the 1918 ballad was Robert A. King (1862-1932) using the pseudonym Mary Earl. Originally the melody was a waltz without words. In its instrumental guise the great violinist Fritz Kreisler recorded it several times.

The words:

Long, long ago,
Someone I know
Had a little red canoe
In it room for only two
Love found its start,
Then in my heart
And like a flower grew. [*chorus*]

Chorus

Drifting with the current down a moonlit stream
While above the Heavens in their glory gleam
And the stars on high
Twinkle in the sky
Seeming in a Paradise of love divine
Dreaming of a pair of eyes that looked in mine
Beautiful Ohio, in dreams again I see
Visions of what used to be.

OKLAHOMA

Oklahoma!: The title song and finishing number of the superlative 1943 musical *Oklahoma!,* this sweeping and rousing composition is perhaps the most brilliant of the official state songs. The musical was the first of several great collaborations of the incomparable duo of Richard Rodgers (1902-1979) and Oscar Hammerstein II (1895-1960).

OREGON

Oregon, My Oregon: With the opening lines "Land of the Empire Builders, Land of the Golden West," this 1920 composition is a very proud song. Officially adopted as the state song in 1927, the words were by J.A. Buchanan and the music was by Henry B. Murtaugh.

The words:

Land of the Empire Builders,
Land of the Golden West;
Conquered and held by freemen,
Fairest and the best.
Onward and upward ever,
Forward on and on;
Hail to thee, Land of Heroes, My Oregon.

PENNSYLVANIA

Pennsylvania: Although Edward Khoury (1916-) and Ronnie Bonner (Aaron J. Bonawitz) (1920?-1991), wrote other songs including "Hook, Line and Sinker" which was used in the 1956 movie *Don't Knock the Rock,* "Pennsylvania" is probably their most important composition. Khoury wrote the words and Bonner wrote the music for this 1966 song, which became the official state song in 1990.

The words:

Pennsylvania, Pennsylvania,
Mighty is your name,
Steeped in glory and tradition
Object of acclaim,
Where brave men fought the foe of freedom,
Tyranny decried,
'Til the bell of independence filled the countryside.
Pennsylvania, Pennsylvania,
May your future be filled with honor everlasting as your history.

Pennsylvania, Pennsylvania,
Blessed by God's own hand,
Birthplace of a mighty nation,
Keystone of the land.
Where first our country's flag unfolded,
Freedom to proclaim,
May the voices of tomorrow glorify your name.
Pennsylvania, Pennsylvania,
May your future be filled with honor everlasting as your history.

RHODE ISLAND

Rhode Island March Song: With much pride, this official state song not only proclaims its significant historical role in the colonial and revolutionary periods of the United States, but also that it is the smallest state in physical size. Written in 1940 by T. Clarke Brown, such charming candor makes this a most interesting composition.

The words:

Here's to you, belov'd Rhode Island,
With your Hills and Ocean Shore,
We are proud to hail you 'Rhody'
And your patriots of yore.
First to claim your Independence,
Great your heritage and fame,
The smallest State in all the Union,
We will glorify your name!

SOUTH CAROLINA

Carolina: Published in 1909, the words of this rousing official state song were by Henry Timrod (1828-1867) and the music was by Anne Curtis Burgess. Another state song of significance is "Stand Tall for South Carolina," with words and music by Nelle McMaster Sprott, which was composed in 1969 to honor the state's tricentennial.

The words:

The despot treads thy sacred sands,
Thy pines give shelter to his bands,
Thy sons stand by with idle hands,
Carolina! Carolina!
He breathes at ease thy airs of balm,
He scorns the lances of thy palm;
Oh, who shall break thy craven calm,
Carolina! Carolina!
Thy ancient fame is growing dim,

A spot is on thy garment's rim;
Give to the winds thy battle hymn,
Carolina! Carolina!

Call on thy children of the hill,
Wake swamp and river, coast and rill,
Rouse all thy strength and all thy skill,
Carolina! Carolina!
Cite wealth and science, trade and art,
Touch with thy fire the cautious mart,
And pour thee through the people's heart,
Carolina! Carolina!
Till even the coward spurns his fears,
And all thy fields and fens and meres
Shall bristle like thy palm with spears,
Carolina! Carolina!

Hold up the glories of the dead;
Say how thy elder children bled,
And point to Eutaw's battle-bed,
Carolina! Carolina!
Tell how the patriot's soul was tried,
And what his dauntless breast defied;
How Rutledge ruled and Laurens died,
Carolina! Carolina!
Cry! till thy summons, heard at last,
Shall fall like Marion's bugle-blast
Re-echoed from the haunted past,
Carolina! Carolina!

I hear a murmur as of waves
That grope their way through sunless caves,
Like bodies struggling in their graves,
Carolina! Carolina!
And now it deepens; slow and grand
It swells, as, rolling to the land,
An ocean broke upon the strand,
Carolina! Carolina!
Shout! let it reach the startled Huns!

And roar with all thy festal guns!
It is the answer of thy sons,
Carolina! Carolina!

They will not wait to hear thee call;
From Sachem's Head to Sumpter's wall
Resounds the voice of hut and hall,
Carolina! Carolina!
No! thou hast not a stain, they say,
Or none save what the battle day
Shall wash in seas of blood away,
Carolina! Carolina!
Thy skirts indeed the foe may part,
Thy robe be pierced with sword and dart,
They shall not touch thy noble heart,
Carolina! Carolina!

Ere thou shalt own the tyrant's thrall
Ten times ten thousand men must fall;
Thy corpse may hearken to his call,
Carolina! Carolina!
When, by thy bier, in mournful throngs
The women chant thy mortal wrongs,
'Twill be their own funereal songs,
Carolina! Carolina!
From thy dead breast by ruffians trod
No helpless child shall look to God;
All shall be safe beneath thy sod,
Carolina! Carolina!

Girt with such wills to do and bear,
Assured in right, and mailed in prayer,
Thou wilt not bow thee to despair,
Carolina! Carolina!
Throw thy bold banner to the breeze!
Front with thy ranks the threatening seas
Like thine own proud armorial trees,
Carolina! Carolina!
Fling down thy gauntlet to the Huns,

And roar thy challenge from thy guns;
Then leave the future to thy sons,
Carolina! Carolina!

SOUTH DAKOTA

South Dakota, My Dakota: This upbeat unofficial song was created to celebrate the centennial of South Dakota in 1989. The South Dakota Bandmasters Association and the South Dakota Arts Council commissioned Bonnie Becker Cacavas to write the words and John Cacavas (1930-) to compose the music.

Hail! South Dakota: With the expansive opening line "Hail! South Dakota, a great state of the land," and a lively march tune, this is a very appropriate official song for a state with a colorful history. Published in 1943, the composition by Deecort Hamitt was the winner of a state song contest.

The words:

Hail! South Dakota,
A great state of the land,
Health, wealth and beauty,
That's what makes her grand;
She has her Black Hills,
And mines with gold so rare,
And with her scen'ry,
No state can compare.

Come where the sun shines,
And where life's worth your while,
You won't be here long,
'Till you'll wear a smile;
No state's so healthy,
And no folk quite so true,
To South Dakota
We all welcome you.

Hail! South Dakota,
The state we love the best,
Land of our fathers,
Builders of the west;
Home of the Badlands,
And Rushmore's ageless shrine,
Black Hills and prairies,
Farmland and sunshine.

TENNESSEE

When It's Iris Time in Tennessee: One of five official state songs, this composition by Willa Waid Newman (or Willa Mae Waid) was written and adopted in 1935. Other state songs are "My Homeland Tennessee" (1925) by Nell Grayson Taylor and Roy Lamont Smith, "Tennessee Waltz" (1948) by Redd Stewart and Pee Wee King, "My Tennessee" (1932) by Frances Hannah Tranum, and "Rocky Top" (1967) by Boudleaux and Felice Bryant.

Tennessee Waltz: A fine blend of Nashville country-western earthiness and Viennese gracefulness, "Tennessee Waltz" was created by Redd Stewart and Pee Wee King (1914-) in 1948. After becoming a top hit in the early 1950s, mostly because of an immensely popular recording by Patti Page, the piece was adopted as the fourth official song of the state.

I Hear You Calling Me, Tennessee: This 1914 song features words by Powell I. Ford and music by Ray Russell.

The words:

Where it's summer time always
Where the birds in the trees
Keep the rolling hills ringing,
With their melodies
There's a voice that keeps whis'pring
Are you coming to me
Far, far away,
In fancy I stray,
To beautiful Tennesee. [*refrain*]

Ev'ry bloom in the garden
Ev'ry leaf on the tree
Ev'ry breeze seems to whisper,
Sunny Tennesee
And the murmuring river
On its way to the sea
Pauses to say,
I'll bear you away,
To beautiful Tennesee. [*refrain*]

Refrain

I hear you calling me, Tennesee,
Soft breezes blow,
And it seems to me,
I see the blossoms on the apple tree
Why I can even hear the droning of a bee
Just like a beautiful melody
Your voice whispers come back to me,
I love you, my own land,
I'm lonesome, dear Homeland,
Just to be near you,
And I can hear you calling me, Tennesee.

TEXAS

Texas, Our Texas: The opening lines of this official song, "Texas, our Texas! All hail the mighty state!," seem very fitting for a state of very large size, scope, and reputation. These far from modest sentiments were penned in 1925 by Gladys Yoakum Wright and William J. Marsh, and set to a melody by Marsh.

The Eyes of Texas: The lyrics for this proud and sweeping song were created in 1903 by John Lang Sinclair (1880-1947) who was associated with the University of Texas at Austin. The familiar melody is from "I've Been Working on the Railroad," an anonymous piece first published in 1894 in a collection of Princeton University songs.

The Yellow Rose of Texas: This song dates from 1858 and was apparently a minstrel tune. The composer, except for his initials ("J.K."), is unknown. Perhaps more than any state song (though this is, of course, an unofficial state song), the words currently sung are quite different from the original lyrics. The present authors have modified the lyrics to fit with current practice (eliminating "darky" and "yellow rose of color"), though "beats the belles of Tennessee" remains.

The words:

There's a yellow rose of Texas that I am going to see,
No other fellow knows her, nobody else but me;
She cried so when I left her, it like to broke my heart,
And if I ever find her we never more will part. [*chorus*]

Where the Rio Grande is flowing, and the starry skies are bright,
She walks along the river in the quiet summer night;
She thinks if I remember, when we parted long ago,
I promised to come back again, and not to leave her so. [*chorus*]

Oh! Now I'm going to find her, for my heart is full of woe,
And we'll sing the song together, that we sung so long ago;
We'll play the banjo gaily, and we'll sing the songs of yore,
And the yellow rose of Texas shall be mine for evermore. [*chorus*]

Chorus

She's the sweetest little rosebud this fellow ever knew,
Her eyes are bright as diamonds, they sparkle like the dew,
You may talk about your Dearest May, and sing of Rosa Lee,
But the yellow rose of Texas beats the belles of Tennessee.

UTAH

Utah, We Love Thee: Written in 1895 to help celebrate the state's admission into the Union in 1896, the song was actually officially adopted twice, in 1917 and 1937. Evan Stephens (1854-), who emigrated from Wales to Utah with his parents in 1866, wrote both the words and music of this uplifting composition.

The words:

Land of the mountains high,
Utah, we love thee!
Land of the sunny sky,
Utah, we love thee!
Far in the glorious west,
Throned on the mountain's crest,
In robes of statehood dressed,
Utah, we love thee!

Columbia's newest star,
Utah, we love thee!
Thy lustre shines afar,
Utah, we love thee!
Bright in our banner's blue,
Among her sisters true,
She proudly comes to view,
Utah, we love thee!

Land of the Pioneers,
Utah, we love thee!
Grow with the coming years,
Utah, we love thee!
With wealth and peace in store,
To fame and glory soar,
God guarded evermore,
Utah, we love thee!

VERMONT

Hail, Vermont!: Josephine Hovey Perry, a Barre, Vermont music teacher born in Quebec, submitted this song to a state committee established in 1937 to choose an official song. Out of over a hundred songs, Mrs. Perry's was selected and became the official song in 1938.

The words:

Hail to Vermont!
Lovely Vermont!
Hail to Vermont so fearless!
Sing we a song!
Sing loud and long!
To our little state so peerless!
Green are her hills,
Clear are her rills,
Fair are her lakes and rivers and valleys:
Blue are her skies,
Peaceful she lies,
But when roused to a call she speedily rallies. [*chorus*]

Proud of Vermont,
Lovely Vermont,
Proud of her charm and beauty;
Proud of her name,
Proud of her fame,
We're proud of her sense of duty;
Proud of her past,
Proud first and last,
Proud of her lands and proud of her waters:
Her men are true,
Her women too,
We're proud of her sons and proud of her daughters. [*chorus*]

Chorus

Hail to Vermont!
Dear old Vermont!
Our love for you is great.
We cherish your name,
We laud! We acclaim!
Our own Green Mountain State.

VIRGINIA

Carry Me Back to Old Virginia: In addition to being Virginia's official state song for many years until it lost its official status early in 1997, this 1878 composition was a sentimental favorite in the popular music scene for decades. Its creator, African-American composer James A. Bland (1854-1911), wrote about 700 songs in all, including the old dance standard, "Oh, Them Golden Slippers" (1879) and the smooth ballad "In the Evening by the Moonlight" (1879). When the Virginia legislature adopted this song as the official state song in 1940 the word "Virginny" was changed to "Virginia."

The words, with "Virginny" changed to "Virginia" and "darky" changed to "wand'rer:":

Carry me back to old Virginia,
There's where the cotton and the corn and taters grow,
There's where the birds warble sweet in the springtime,
There's where this old wand'rer's heart longs to go.
There's where I labored so hard for old Massa,
Day after day in the yellow corn,
No place on earth do I love more sincerely
Than old Virginia, the state where I was born. [*chorus*]

Carry me back to old Virginia,
There let me live until I decay,
Long by the old Dismal Swamp have I wandered,
There's where this old wand'rer's life will pass away,
Massa and Missis have long gone before me,
Soon we will meet on that bright and golden shore,
There we'll be happy and free from all sorrow,
There's where we'll meet and we'll never part no more. [*chorus*]

Chorus

Carry me back to old Virginia,
There's where the cotton and the corn and taters grow,
There's where the birds warble sweet in the springtime,
There's where the old wand'rer's heart longs to go.

WASHINGTON

Washington My Home: Adopted in 1959 as the official state song, replacing "Washington Beloved" which had been unofficially adopted in 1909, this sentimental composition of uncertain date was written by Helen Davis of South Bend, Washington. Mrs. Davis was well known in the state as a song writer and creator of musical productions.

The words:

This is my country; God gave it to me;
I protect it, ever keep it free,
Small towns and cities rest here in the sun,
Filled with our laughter, "Thy will be done."

Washington, my home;
Wherever I may roam;
The is my land, my native land,
Washington, my home.
Our verdant forest green,
Caressed by silvery stream;
From mountain peak to fields of wheat.
Washington, my home.

There's peace you feel and understand
In this, our own beloved land.
We greet the day with head held high,
And forward ever is our cry.
We'll happy ever be
As people always free.
For you and me a destiny;
Washington, my home.

Washington Beloved: In 1909, the state legislature unofficially adopted this 1907 composition as the state song. The words were by Edmond S. Meany (1862-1935), professor at the University of Washington, and the music was by Reginald De Koven (1859-1920), a famous composer who created the opera *Robin Hood*. In 1959, "Washington, My Home" replaced it as the official song.

WEST VIRGINIA

The West Virginia Hills: This song, with late 19th century words by Ellen King and music of uncertain date by H.E. Engle, became the official state song in 1963. Other state songs are "This Is My West Virginia" and "West Virginia My Home Sweet Home."

The words:

Oh, the West Virginia hills!
How majestic and how grand,
With their summits bathed in glory,
Like our Prince Immanuel's land!
Is it any wonder then,
That my heart with rapture thrills,
As I stand once more with loved ones
On those West Virginia hills? [*chorus*]

Oh, the West Virginia hills!
Where my girlhood's hours were passed,
Where I often wander'd lonely,
And the future tried to cast;
Many are our visions bright
Which the future ne'er fulfills;
But how sunny were my daydreams
On those West Virginia hills! [*chorus*]

Oh, the West Virginia hills!
How unchang'd they seem to stand,
With their summits pointed skyward
To the Great Almighty's Land!
Many changes I can see,
Which my heart with sadness fills,
But no changes can be noticed
In those West Virginia hills! [*chorus*]

Oh, the West Virginia hills!
I must bid you now adieu,
In my home beyond the mountains

I shall ever dream of you;
In the evening time of life,
If my Father only wills,
I shall still behold the vision
Of those West Virginia hills! [*chorus*]

Chorus

O the hills,
Beautiful hills,
How I love those West Virginia hills.
If o'er sea or land I roam,
Still I'll think of happy home
And the friends among the West Virginia hills.

WISCONSIN

On, Wisconsin: This was originally written in 1909 as a superb college song for the University of Wisconsin by composer William Thomas Purdy (1883-1918) and lyricist Carl Beck. The lyrics were changed in 1913 by J.S. Hubbard and Charles D. Rosa to make them suitable for a state song, but the revised version didn't become official until 1959.

The words:

On, Wisconsin! On, Wisconsin!
Grand old badger state!
We, thy loyal sons and daughters,
Hail thee, good and great.
On, Wisconsin! On, Wisconsin!
Champion of the right,
"Forward," our motto—
God will give thee might!

WYOMING

The Wyoming State Song: Written in 1903 by lyricist Charles E. Winter and composer Earle R. Clemens, this composition was immediately but unofficially declared the state song. Despite its official sounding title, however, the legislature adopted a variant of this, with the title "Wyoming," as the official song.

The words:

In the far and mighty West,
Where the crimson sun seeks rest,
There's a growing splendid State that lies above
On the breast of this great land;
Where the massive Rockies stand,
There's Wyoming young and strong, the State I love! [*chorus*]

In thy flowers wild and sweet,
Colors rare and perfumes meet;
There's the columbine so pure, the daisy too,
Wild the rose and red it springs,
White the button and its rings,
Thou art loyal for they're red and white and blue. [*chorus*]

Where thy peaks with crowned head.
Rising till the sky they wed,
Sit like snow queens ruling wood and stream and plain;
Neath thy granite bases deep,
Neath thy bosom's broadened sweep,
Lie riches that have gained and brought thee fame. [*chorus*]

Other treasures thou dost hold,
Men and women thou dost mould;
True and earnest are the lives that thou dost raise,
Strength thy children thou dost teach,
Nature's truth thou givst to each,
Free and noble are thy workings and thy ways. [*chorus*]

In the nation's banner free
There's one star that has for me
A radiance pure and a splendor like the sun;
Mine it is, Wyoming's star,
Home it leads me near or far;
O Wyoming! all my heart and love you've won! [*chorus*]

Chorus

Wyoming, Wyoming!
Land of sunlight clear!
Wyoming, Wyoming!
Land that we hold so dear!
Wyoming, Wyoming!
Precious art thou and thine;
Wyoming, Wyoming!
Beloved State of mine!

Wyoming: Using the same excellent lyrics created by Charles E. Winter in 1903 for the unofficial state song ("The Wyoming State Song"), George E. Knapp, a professor of music at the University of Wyoming, created a good march tempo setting in 1920. Also known as "Wyoming March Song," it became the state song in 1955.

SONG TEXTS

Alabama

Julia S. Tutwiler

Edna Gockel Gussen

Al - a -bam - a, Al - a-bam -a, we will aye be true to thee,

From thy South - ern shores where grow - eth By the sea thy

o - range tree. To thy North - ern vale where flow - eth

Deep and blue thy Ten - nes - see, Al - a-bam - a,

Al - a-bam - a, we will aye be true to thee.

Public Domain

Arizona March Song

Margaret Rowe Clifford

Maurice Blumenthal

Come to this land of sun - shine, To this land where life is young, Where the wide, wide world is wait - ing, The songs that will now be sung. Where the

gold-en sun is flam-ing In-to warm, white, shin-ing day, And the

sons of men are blaz-ing Their price-less right of way.   Sing the

dolce

Chorus   *Dolce with expression*

song that's in your hearts,   Sing   of the great South-west,   Thank

God, for Ar - i - zon - a In splen - did sun - shine dressed, For thy

beau - ty and thy grand-eur, For thy re - gal robes so sheen, We hail thee Ar - i -

zon - a Our god - dess and our queen. Sing the queen.

Arkansas

Eva Ware Barnett

days, Where I roamed through the woods and the

mea - dows, By the mill and the brook that

plays; Where the roses are in bloom, And the

sweet mag - nol - ia too, Where the   jas - mine is white, And the

fields are vio - let blue, There a   wel - come a - waits   all her

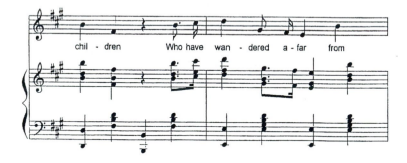

chil - dren   Who have wan - dered a - far   from

Chorus

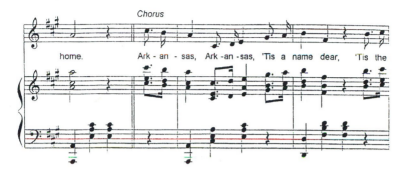

home. Ark - an - sas, Ark -an -sas, 'Tis a name dear, 'Tis the

place I call "Home, Sweet Home;" Ark - an - sas Ark -an -sas, I sa-

lute thee, From thy shel -ter no more I'll roam.

The Arkansas Traveler

On a lone-ly road quite long a-go   A trav'-ler trod with
fid-dle and a bow: While ram-bling thru the coun-try rich and grand,   He
quick-ly sensed the mag-ic and the beau-ty of the land.

Public Domain

For the Won - der State we'll sing a song, And lift our voic - es loud and long. For the Won - der State we'll shout Hur - rah! And praise the op - por - tu - ni - ties we find in Ar - kan - sas.

I Love You, California

F. B. Silverwood

A. F. Frankenstein

CHORUS (Trio)

Where the snow crowned Gold-en Si- er - ras____ Keep their watch o'er the val - leys bloom,____ It is there I would be in our land by the sea, Ev -'ry breeze bearing rich per -

fume._____ It is here na-ture gives of her rar-est It is

Home Sweet Home to Me,_____ And I know when I die I shall

breathe my last sigh For my sun-ny Cal - i - forn - ia.

Where the Columbines Grow

A. J. Fynn

trop-ic stars shine; __ Where the scream of the bold moun-tain ea-gle Re -

sponds to the notes of the dove___ Is the pur-ple robed West, the land that is

best. The pi-o-neer land that we love.___ 'Tis the land where the

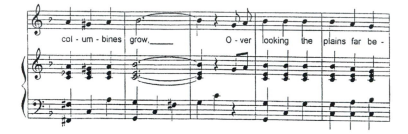

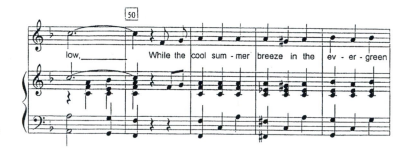

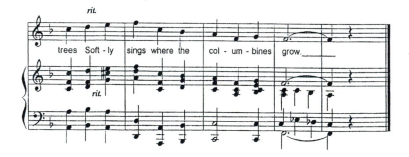

Yankee Doodle

Yank - ee Doo - dle went to town, Rid -ing on a po - ny,

Stuck a fea -ther in his hat, and called it ma - ca - ro - ni.

Chorus

Yank - ee Doo - dle keep it up, Yank - ee Doo - dle Dan - dy,

Mind the mus - ic and the step, And with the folks be han - dy.

Our Delaware

George B. Hynson

Will M. S. Brown

Oh the hills of dear New Cas-tle, And the smil-ing vales be-tween, When the corn is all in tas-sel, And the mead-ow lands are green; Where the cat-tle crop the

Delaware State Archives

clo - ver, And its breath is in the air, While the

sun is shin - ing o - ver Our be - lov - ed Del - a - ware.

CHORUS *Tempo di March*

Oh, our Del - a - ware! Our be - lov - ed Del - a - ware! For the

sun is shin-ing o-ver our be-lov-ed Del-a-ware,

Oh! our Del-a-ware! Our be-lov-ed Del-a-ware! Here's the

loy-al son that pledg-es, Faith to good old Del-a-ware.

Old Folks at Home

Stephen Foster

Moderato

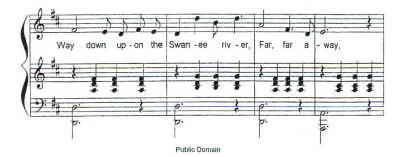

Way down up-on the Swan-ee riv-er, Far, far a-way,

There's where my heart is turn-ing ev-er, There's where the old folks stay.

All up and down the whole cre-a-tion, Sad-ly I roam,

Still long-ing for the old plan-ta-tion, And for the old folks at home.

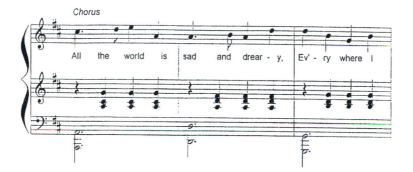

Chorus

All the world is sad and drear - y, Ev' - ry where I

roam, Oh! peo - ple how my heart grows wear - y,

Far from the old folks at home.

Georgia

Robert Loveman

Lollie Belle Wylie

Geor - gia land of our de - light, Ha - ven of the

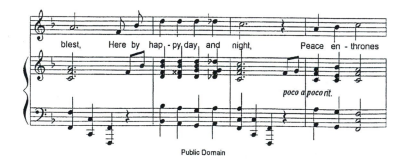

blest, Here by hap - py day and night, Peace en - thrones

poco a poco rit.

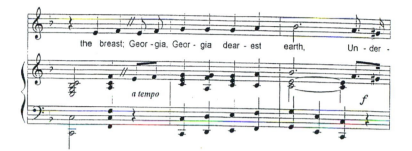

the breast; Geor - gia. Geor - gia dear - est earth, Un - der -

neath the blue, Clime that ev - er giv - eth

birth To the brave and true.

Hawai'i Pono'i

David Kalakaua

H. Berger

Public Domain

Here We Have Idaho

Albert J. Tompkins (verses)
McKinley Helm (chorus)

Sallie Hume-Douglas

You've heard of the won-ders our land does pos-sess, Its beau-ti-ful val-leys and hills__ The ma-jes-tic for-ests where na-ture a-bounds, We love ev-ery no-ok and rill.

Chorus

And here we have I-da-ho____ Win-ning her way to fame____

Music: Public Domain   Words: By Permission of the University of Idaho

Sil-ver and gold in the sun-light blaze, And ro-mance lies in her name__

Sing - ing we're sing-ing of you, And proud-ly too, All our lives

thru, We'll go sing - ing sing-ing of you, sing-ing of I - da - ho____

Illinois

C. H. Chamberlin

Archibald Johnston ("Baby Mine")

By thy riv-ers gen -tly flow-ing, Il-li-nois, Il-li-nois, O'er thy prai-ries ver-dant grow -ing, Il -li -nois, Il -li - nois, Comes an ech -o on the breeze, Rus -tling thro' the leaf- y trees, and its mel -low tones are these, Il -li - nois, Il -li - nois, And its mel -low tones are these, Il -li - nois!

Public Domain

On the Banks of the Wabash, Far Away

Paul Dresser

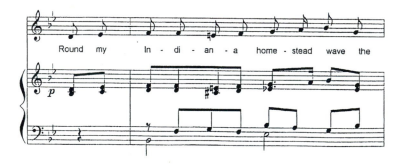

Round   my   In - di - an - a   home - stead   wave   the

corn - field, In the dis - tance loom the wood - lands clear and

cool_____ Of - ten times my thoughts re - vert to scenes of

child - hood, Where I first re - ceived my les - sons, na - ture's

school._____ But one thing there is mis - sing in the

pic - ture, With - out her face it seems so in - com -

plete._____ I long to see my moth - er in the

door - way. As she stood there years a - go, her boy to

Refrain

greet!_____ Oh, the

moon - light's fair to -night a -long the Wa - bash, From the

fields there comes the breath of new mown hay.__ Thro the

syc - a - mores the can - dle lights are gleam - ing, On the

banks of the Wa - bash, far a - way._____

Iowa Corn Song

Ray W. Lockard
George Hamilton

Edward Riley

Let's

sing of Grand old I - O -WAY, Yo - ho, yo-ho, yo - ho, Our

love is strong -er ev - 'ry day, Yo - ho, yo - ho, yo - ho. So

Public Domain

come a -long and join the throng, Sev -'ral hun -dred thou-sand strong,

As you come just sing this song, Yo - ho, yo - ho, yo-ho. We're from

CHORUS

I - o - way   I - o - way.

State of all the land. Joy on ev-'ry hand. We're from

I - o - way, I - o - way.

1.

That's where the tall corn grows. We're from grows.

2.

The Song of Iowa

S. H. M. Byers

"O Tannenbaum"

You ask what land I love the best, I-o-wa, 'tis I-o-wa, The fair-est State of all the west, I-o-wa, O! I-o-wa. From yon-der Mis-sis-sip-pi's stream To where Mis-sou-ri's wa-ters gleam, O! fair it is as po-et's dream, I-o-wa, in I-o-wa.

Home on the Range

Brewster Higley

Dan Kelley

Oh give me a home where the buf - fa - lo roam Where the deer and the an - te - lope play Where sel - dom is heard a dis - cour - ag - ing word And the skies are not cloud - y all day

Chorus

Home,   home on the   range   Where the

deer   and the   lan - te - lope   play   Where

sel - dom is   heard   a dis - cour - ag - ing   word   And the

skies are not   cloud - y   all   day

My Old Kentucky Home, Good-Night!

Stephen Foster

The sun shines bright in the old Ken-tuck-y home, 'Tis sum-mer the peo-ple are gay, The corn top's ripe and the

mea-dow's in the bloom While the birds make mus - ic all the

day.   The young folks roll on the

lit - tle ca - bin floor,   All mer - ry,   all hap - py   and

bright: By'n   by   Hard   Times   comes a

knock-ing at the door, Then my old Ken-tuck-y Home, good night!

Chorus

Weep no more, my la-dy, oh! weep no more to-

day! We will sing one song For the

old Ken-tuck-y home, For the old Ken-tuck-y home, far a way.

My Louisiana

Howard A. Winburn

Henry Wehrmann

Public Domain

Birds sing their sweet-est songs That's where my heart be-longs

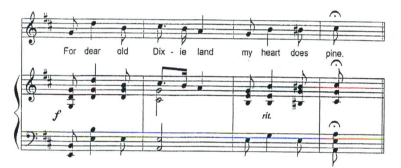

For dear old Dix-ie land my heart does pine.

Refrain

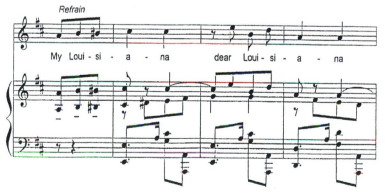

My Loui-si-a-na dear Loui-si-a-na

State of Maine

Roger Vinton Snow

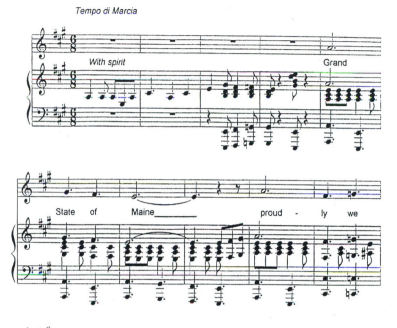

Reprinted by permission

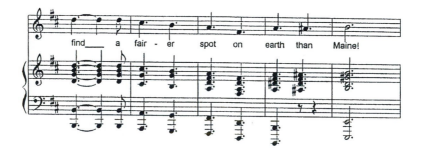

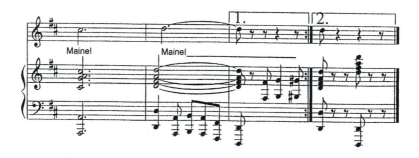

Maryland, My Maryland!

James Ryder Randall

O Tannenbaum
arranged by C. E.

All Hail to Massachusetts

Arthur J Marsh

All hail to Mas - sa - chu - setts, the land of the free and the brave! For Bun - ker hill and Charles - town and flag we love to wave: For

Public Domain

My Michigan

Oliver D. Salisbury

I have wan-dered down in sun-ny Miss - is - sip - pi, Where the sug - ar - cane and cot - ton blos - somes

grow.   I have   heard the   peo - ple sing   in Al - a -

bam - a   And made love   to dus - ky maids   in   I - da

- ho.   But there's just one spot that holds   af -

fec - tion, With its Murm' - ring pines be - side the in - land

sea, In Mich - i - gan, My Mich - i - gan, The

on - ly land in all the world for me.

L.H.

Back to my boy-hood I wan - der, My sweet-heart is

wait-ing once more By the moss cov - ered pine in the

door yard, Down by old Mich - i - gan's shore

Hail! Minnesota

Truman E. Rickard
Arthur E. Upson

Truman E. Rickard

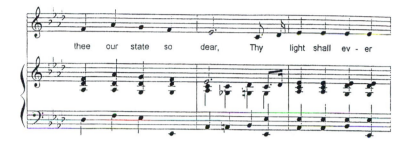

thee our state so dear, Thy light shall ev - er

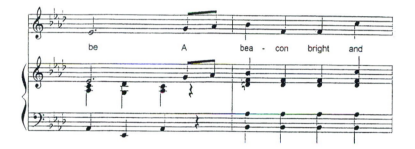

be A bea - con bright and

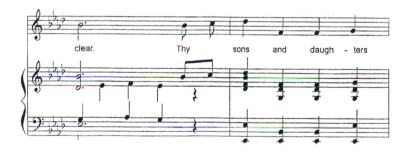

clear. Thy sons and daugh - ters

Mississippi Days

Ballard MacDonald

Al Piantadosi

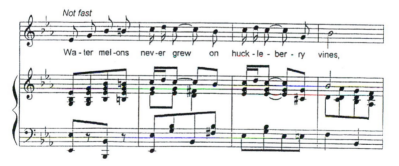

Public Domain

Chorus

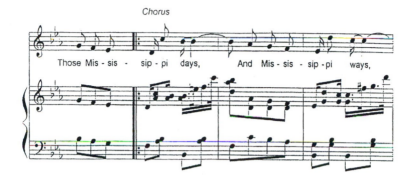

Those Mis - sis - sip - pi days, And Mis - sis - sip - pi ways,

Those old plan - ta - tion songs, While steam - boats

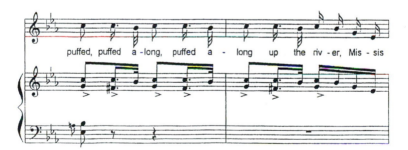

puffed, puffed a - long, puffed a - long up the riv - er, Mis - sis

-sip-pi   nights,   And Mis-sis-sip-pi   sights,   Oh! how my

heart is burn-ing, Thoughts are turn-ing,   I'm yearn-ing, How I miss those

Mis   - sis-sip-pi days,   Those Mis-sis   days.

-sip -pi   nights,   And Mis -sis -sip -pi   sights,   Oh! how my

heart is burn -ing, Thoughts are turn -ing, I'm yearn -ing, How I miss   those

Mis - sis -sip -pi days,   Those Mis -sis   days.

Missouri Waltz

J. R. Shannon

Slowly and dreamily

Frederic Knight Logan

Hush - a - bye, ma ba - by, slum - ber time is com-in' soon; Rest yo' head up - on my breast while Mom - my hums a tune; The sand - man is call - in' where shad-ows are

Hear that mourn - ful mel - o - dy It just haunts you the

whole day long, And you wan - der in dreams back to

Dix - ie, it seems, When you hear that old time song.

Hush - a - bye, ma ba - by, go to sleep on Mom - my's

knee, Jour - ney back to Dix - ie - land in dreams a - gain with

me; It seems like your Mom - my is there once a -

gain, And the old folks were strum - min' that same old re -

frain. 'Way down in Mis - sou - ri where I learned this lul - la -

.by, When the stars were blink-in' and the moon was climb-in'

high, Seems I hear voic - es low, as in days long a - go, Sing - in'

hush - a - bye.

Montana

Charles C. Cohan

Joseph E. Howard

Tempo di Marcia

Tell me of that Trea-sure State Stor-y al-ways new, Tell of its beau-ties grand And its hearts so true.

Moun - tains of sun - set fire The land I love the best

Let me grasp the hand of

one From out the gold - en West.

Mon - ta - na, Mon - ta - na, Glo - ry of the

Beautiful Nebraska

Jim Fras
Guy G. Miller

Jim Fras

Beau - ti - ful Ne - bra - ska, peace-ful prai - rie land,

Land with ma-ny ri - vers and the hills of sand; Dark green val - leys

cra - dled in the earth,   Rain and sun - shine bring a - bun - dant birth.

Beau - ti - ful Ne - bra - ska,   as you look a - round, You will find a rain - bow

rea - ching to the ground;   All these won - ders   by the Mas-ter's hand

Beau-ti-ful Ne-bra-ska land. We are so proud of this state where we live, There is no place that has so much to give.

Beau - ti -ful Ne -bra-ska,   as you look a - round,   you will find a rain - bow

rea -ching to the ground;   All these won - ders   by the Mas -ter's hand;

Beau - ti - ful   Ne - bra - ska   land.

Old New Hampshire

John F. Holmes

Maurice Hoffmann

With a skill that knows no meas-ure, From the gold-en store of

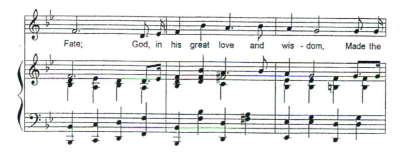

Fate; God, in his great love and wis-dom, Made the

Public Domain

rug - ged Gran - ite   State;   Made the lakes, the fields, the

for -ests;   Made the riv - ers and   the   rills;   Made the

bub - bling, crys - tal foun -tain Of New Hamp -shire's Gran -ite   Hills.

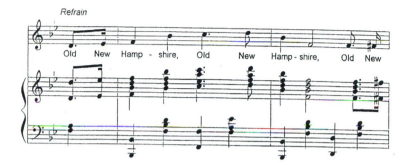

Refrain

Old New Hamp - shire, Old New Hamp - shire, Old New

Hamp - shire grand and great, We will sing of Old New

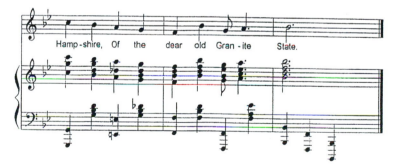

Hamp - shire, Of the dear old Gran - ite State.

Ode to New Jersey

O Tannenbaum

The roll-ing wave is on thy shore, Jer-sey-land, my Jer-sey-land! A-loft thine az-ure moun-tains soar, Jer-sey-land, my Jer-sey-land! Hill-top and vale, low ly-ing plain, Thy pines, thy streams with murm'-ring strain, These ne'er will let thy beau-ty wane, Jer-sey-land, my Jer-sey-land!

O, Fair New Mexico

Elizabeth Garrett

Under a sky of a - zure, Where balm - y bre - ezes blow; Kissed by the gold - en sun - shine,

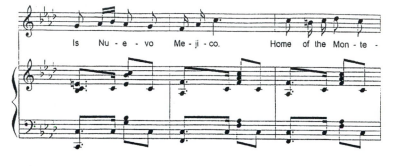

Is Nu - e - vo Me - ji - co.   Home of the Mon - te -

zu - ma,   With fie - ry heart a - glow,

State of the deeds his - tor - ic,   Is Nue - vo Me - ji - co.

The Sidewalks of New York

Charles B. Lawlor & James W. Blake

Down in front of Ca - sey's,_____ Old brown wood - en stoop,_____ On a sum - mer's eve - ning,

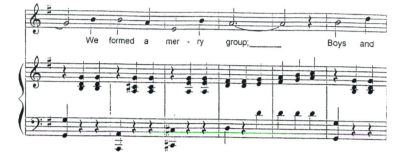

We formed a mer - ry group;_____ Boys and

girls to - geth - er,_____ We would sing and waltz,_____

while the "Gin - nie" played the or - gan on the side - walks

Boys and girls to - geth - er,_____ Me and

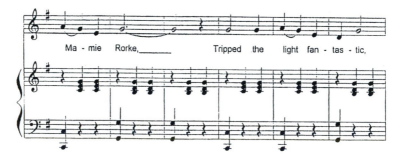

Ma - mie Rorke,_____ Tripped the light fan - tas - tic,

On the side - walks of New York._____

The Old North State

William Gaston

Traditional melody arranged by Mrs. E. E. Randolph

With spirit

Car - o - li - na! Car - o - lin - a! heaven's - bless - ings at - tend her, While we live we will cher - ish, pro - tect and de - fend her, Tho' the scom - er may sneer at and wit - lings de -

fame her, Still our hearts swell with glad - ness when

Chorus

ev - er we name her. Hur - rah! Hur - rah! the

Old North State for - ev - er, Hur - rah! Hur -

rit.

rah! the good Old North State.

Beautiful Ohio

Ballard MacDonald

Mary Earl

Long, long a-go, Some-one I know

Had a lit-tle red ca-noe

In it on-ly room for two Love found its

Public Domain

glo - ry gleam And the

stars on high_____

Twin - kle in the sky_____

diminuendo

Seem - ing in a Par - a - dise of

Oregon, My Oregon

J. A. Buchanan

Henry B. Murtagh

Land of the Em-pire Build-ers, Land of the Gold-en West;____

Con - quered and held by free-men, Fair-est__ and the

Pennsylvania

Eddie Khoury
Ronnie Bonner

Penn - syl - va - nia, Penn - syl - va - nia, Might - y is your name, Steeped in glo -ry and tra - di - tion Ob - ject of ac -

Public Domain

Rhode Island March Song

T. Clarke Brown

Here's to you, be-lov'd Rhode Is - land With your

Hills and O - cean Shore, We are proud

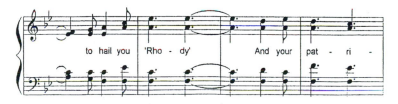

to hail you 'Rho - dy' And your pat - ri -

ots   of   yore.   First to   claim   your in-de-

pen - dence,   Great your her - i - tage and

fame,   The small - est State   in all the

U - nion,   We will glor - i - fy   your   name!

Carolina

Henry Timrod　　　　　　　　　　　　　　　　　Anne Curtis Burgess

The des-pot treads thy sa-cred sands, Thy pines give shel-ter to his bands, Thy sons stand by with i-dle hands, Car-o-lin-a, Car-o-lin-a! He breathes at ease thy airs of balm, He scorns the lan-ces of thy palm;

Oh, who shall break thy cra - ven calm, Car - o -

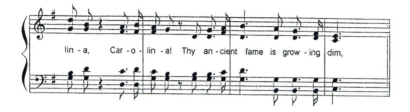

lin - a, Car - o - lin - a! Thy an - cient fame is grow - ing dim,

A spot is on thy gar - ment's rim; Give to the winds thy bat - tle

hymn, Car - o - lin - a, Car - o - lin - a!

Hail! South Dakota

Deecort Hammitt

Snappy march time

Hail! South Da -

ko - ta, A great state of the land,_____

Used by permission of the state of South Dakota

I Hear You Calling Me, Tennessee

Powell I. Ford

Ray Russell

cresc.

Where it's sum-mer time al - ways_____ Where the birds in the

p

trees_____ Keep the roll-ing hills ring - ing,_____ With their mel - o -

beau-ti-ful mel-o-dy your voice whis-pers come back to me, I

love you, my own land, I'm lone - some, dear Home - land,

rit.

Just to be near you, And I can hear you call-ing me, Tenn - e - see.

a tempo

The Yellow Rose of Texas

J.K.

Allegretto

There's a yel - low rose in Tex - as that I am going to see, No

She's the sweet-est lit-tle rose-bud this fel-low ev-er knew, Her

eyes are bright as dia-monds, they spar-kle like the dew, You may

talk a-bout your Dear-est May, and sing of Ros-a Lee, But the

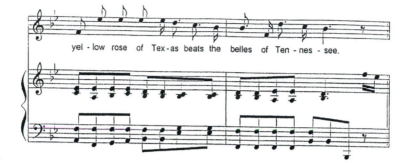

yel - low rose of Tex-as beats the belles of Ten - nes - see.

Utah, We Love Thee

Evan Stephens

Land of the moun-tains high, U -tah, we love thee! Land of the sun - ny sky,

U -tah, we love thee! Far in the glo - rious west, Throned on the moun -tain's crest,

In robes of state -hood dressed, U - tah, we love thee!

Public Domain

Hail, Vermont!

Josephine Hovey Perry

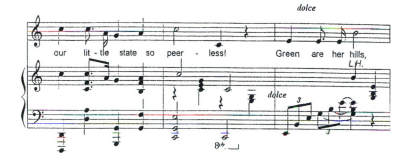

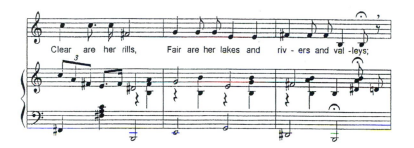

Carry Me Back to Old Virginia

James Bland

There's where the birds war - ble sweet in the spring - time,

There's where this old wand' - rer's heart does long to go.

There's where I la - bored so hard for old Mas - sa,

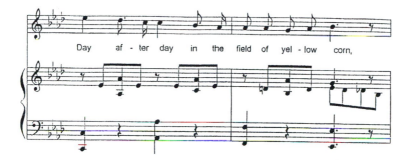

Day af - ter day in the field of yel - low corn,

No place on earth do I love more sin - cere - ly

Than old Vir - gin - ia, the state where I was born.

Washington My Home

Helen Davis
arranged by Stuart Churchill

This is my coun - try; God gave it to me; I will pro - tect it, Ev - er keep it free. Small towns and

cit - ies Rest here in the sun, Filled with our

laugh -ter, Thy will be done. Wash-ing -ton my

home; Where ev- er I may roam; This is my land, my

p   *March tempo*

p

un - der - stand In this, our own be - lov - ed land. We

greet the day with head held high, And for - ward ev - er

is our cry. We'll hap - py ev - er be As peo - ple al - ways

The West Virginia Hills

Ellen King

H. E. Engle

Oh, the West Vir-gin-ia hills! How ma-jes-tic and how grand, With their sum-mits bathed in glo-ry, Like our Prince Im-man-uel's land! Is it a-ny won-der then, That my heart with rap-ture thrills, As I stand once more with loved ones on those

On, Wisconsin!

J. S. Hubbard
C. D. Rosa

W. T. Purdy

On, Wis - con - sin! On, Wis - con - sin! Grand old bad - ger state! We, thy loy - al sons and daugh - ters, Hail thee good and great

Public Domain

On Wis - con - sin! On, Wis - con - sin! Cham - pion

of the right,   "For - ward," our mot - to:

God will give thee might!

Wyoming

C. E. Winter

March tempo

G. E. Knapp

In the far and might - y West, Where the

crim - son sun seeks rest There's a

growing splen - did State that lies a - bove On the

Used by permission of Bailey School & Office Supply

breast   of   this   great   land;   Where   the

mas - sive Rock - ies stand, there's Wy - o - ming young and strong,   the

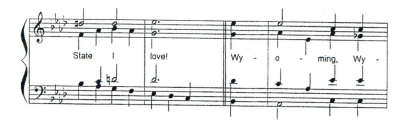

State   I   love!   Wy - o - ming,   Wy -

o - ming!   Land   of   the   sun - light   clear!   Wy -

o - ming, Wy - o - ming! Land that we hold so dear! Wy - o - ming, Wy - o - ming! Prec - ious art thou and thine; Wy - o - ming, Wy -

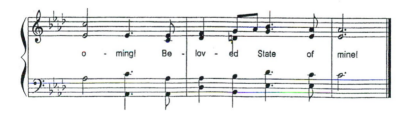

o - ming! Be - lov - ed State of mine!

Bibliographical Note

Most of the information on the songs in this volume was obtained from direct inquiries to the governments of the 50 states. The rest was derived bit by bit from the online OCLC database and various standard reference works, of which only two were used to an appreciable extent. These two were:

1. James J. Fuld, *The Book of World Famous Music: Classical, Popular, and Folk,* 3rd ed., rev. and enlarged (New York: Dover, 1985).
2. Roger Lax and Frederick Smith, *The Great Song Thesaurus,* 2nd ed., updated and expanded (New York: Oxford University Press, 1989).

Besides this volume, there are two other post-World War II collections of state song texts known to be in existence. They are:

1. *State Songs of the United States,* compiled by Judith Petke. (Chicago: Chicago Public Library, 1977).
2. *Fifty Songs–Fifty States: A Song for Every State in the U.S.A.,* compiled, arranged and edited by John W. Schaum (Milwaukee: Schaum Publications, 1982).

Unfortunately, neither of these anthologies are of much value. The Petke collection is only known to be in the Chicago Public Library and therefore is not easily accessible. The Schaum collection is more widely available, but is designed primarily for use in schools. It includes only one verse of each song and little historical data.

Index of Persons

Index of Titles

Haworth
DOCUMENT DELIVERY
SERVICE

This valuable service provides a single-article order form for any article from a Haworth journal.

- *Time Saving:* No running around from library to library to find a specific article.
- *Cost Effective:* All costs are kept down to a minimum.
- *Fast Delivery:* Choose from several options, including same-day FAX.
- *No Copyright Hassles:* You will be supplied by the original publisher.
- *Easy Payment:* Choose from several easy payment methods.

Open Accounts Welcome for . . .
- Library Interlibrary Loan Departments
- Library Network/Consortia Wishing to Provide Single-Article Services
- Indexing/Abstracting Services with Single Article Provision Services
- Document Provision Brokers and Freelance Information Service Providers

---

MAIL or *FAX* THIS ENTIRE ORDER FORM TO:

Haworth Document Delivery Service
The Haworth Press, Inc.
10 Alice Street
Binghamton, NY 13904-1580

or FAX: 1-800-895-0582
or CALL: 1-800-342-9678
9am-5pm EST

PLEASE SEND ME PHOTOCOPIES OF THE FOLLOWING SINGLE ARTICLES:

1) Journal Title: _____
   Vol/Issue/Year: _____ Starting & Ending Pages: _____
   Article Title: _____

2) Journal Title: _____
   Vol/Issue/Year: _____ Starting & Ending Pages: _____
   Article Title: _____

3) Journal Title: _____
   Vol/Issue/Year: _____ Starting & Ending Pages: _____
   Article Title: _____

4) Journal Title: _____
   Vol/Issue/Year: _____ Starting & Ending Pages: _____
   Article Title: _____

(See other side for Costs and Payment Information)

COSTS: Please figure your cost to order quality copies of an article.

1. Set-up charge per article: $8.00 \
                   ($8.00 × number of separate articles)   _____

2. Photocopying charge for each article:

                  1-10 pages: $1.00   _____

                  11-19 pages: $3.00   _____

                  20-29 pages: $5.00   _____

                  30+ pages: $2.00/10 pages   _____

3. Flexicover (optional): $2.00/article   _____

4. Postage & Handling: US: $1.00 for the first article/

                  $.50 each additional article   _____

           Federal Express: $25.00   _____

           Outside US: $2.00 for first article/

                  $.50 each additional article _____

5. Same-day FAX service: $.35 per page   _____

               GRAND TOTAL: _____

METHOD OF PAYMENT: (please check one)

❑ Check enclosed   ❑ Please ship and bill. PO # _____

           (sorry we can ship and bill to bookstores only! All others must pre-pay)

❑ Charge to my credit card: ❑ Visa; ❑ MasterCard; ❑ Discover;

          ❑ American Express;

Account Number: _____ Expiration date:_____

Signature: ✗ _____

Name: _____ Institution: _____

Address: _____

        _____

City: _____ State:_____ Zip:_____

Phone Number: _____ FAX Number: _____

MAIL or *FAX* THIS ENTIRE ORDER FORM TO:

Haworth Document Delivery Service | **or FAX:** 1-800-895-0582 \
The Haworth Press, Inc. | **or CALL:** 1-800-342-9678 \
10 Alice Street | 9am-5pm EST) \
Binghamton, NY 13904-1580

12·22·98 $29.95   B+T